Sea Anemones and Corals

OF BRITAIN AND IRELAND

Second edition

T0339359

Chris Wood

WILD
NATURE
PRESS

Seasearch is a volunteer underwater survey project for recreational
divers. The information they gather is used to increase their
knowledge of the marine environment and contribute towards
its conservation. For further information about Seasearch or to
participate in the project visit the website
www.seasearch.org.uk

First published in 2005 by
Marine Conservation Society
Overross House
Ross Park
Ross-on-Wye
Herefordshire
HR9 7US, UK

Second edition in 2013 by
Wild Nature Press
Winson House
Church Road
Plympton St Maurice
Plymouth
PL7 1NH, UK

Reprinted with amendments 2018

A CIP catalogue record for this book is available from the British Library

ISBN 978-0-9573946-3-6

Printed in Slovakia

10 9 8 7 6 5 4 3

press.princeton.edu

Recommended citation:
Wood, C. 2013. *Sea Anemones and Corals of Britain and Ireland.* Second edition. Wild Nature Press, Plymouth, UK.

Main cover photograph: *Sagartia troglodytes*, Rob Spray. Other cover photographs: Keith Hiscock and Chris Wood.
Title page and opposite: varieties of *Sagartia elegans*, Chris Wood.

Contents

One of Keith Hiscock's images of *Leptopsammia pruvoti* taken at one of his local reefs south of Plymouth.

Foreword

The fascination that exists for sea anemones and corals goes back a long way – to the Victorian naturalists who attended 'out-of-door' classes for the study of marine natural history' and snapped-up copies of books by Philip Henry Gosse, George Tugwell and others on the creatures. It was Gosse's *Actinologia Britannica* that started my fascination with corals in particular – corals in British waters! I had thought that corals were confined to the tropics. So, in the 1960s, I could be seen looking for and finding the species that Gosse had described from the same shores that he had worked around Ilfracombe. And then, diving opened my eyes to the underwater world where, again, sea anemones and especially corals were a highlight for me including making the first record for British waters of the Sunset Coral *Leptopsammia pruvoti* at Lundy in 1969.

It is not surprising that sea anemones and corals are so popular with divers and rockpoolers. They are colourful and exotic. The illustrations of Gosse and, later, T.A. Stephenson in *The British Sea Anemones* are beautiful, whilst the Linnean Society Synopsis on *British Anthozoa* by R. L. Manual is up-to-date and technical. But divers would need something accessible and which was not too technical, especially for the very valuable surveys being undertaken by Seasearch. The earlier edition of the Seasearch *Guide to Sea Anemones and Corals* is always what I reach for first when I need to remind myself of the name for something and, more-often-than-not, it does the job.

The nearly 100 species of sea anemones and corals that occur in shallow waters around Britain and Ireland are a part of the marvelous biodiversity that we have around our shores. The more that we know about their distribution and abundance and the more observations that we make of their biology and any changes in their occurrence, the better placed we are to ensure their continued presence.

Chris Wood exemplifies the long tradition of non-specialists that lead our studies of marine natural history and enrich the lives of divers and rockpoolers curious to know the names of what they are seeing. This new edition of *Sea Anemones and Corals of Britain and Ireland* brings the identification and factual information about each species into one easily understood guide. The photographs, mainly by Chris Wood but also by other talented photographers, 'make' the guide. Enjoy using the book.

Dr Keith Hiscock
Associate Fellow at the Marine Biological Association of the UK

One of the author's images of *Sagartia elegans* taken in the Isle of Man.

The author recording near Lands End.

About the author

Chris Wood was formerly the National Coordinator for Seasearch and has been a keen diver for over fifty years ever since joining the University of London Sub Aqua Club an as undergraduate. He has been involved in observing and recording marine life throughout his diving career and has been involved in the Marine Conservation Society and Seasearch since their inception.

Chris has dived all around Britain and Ireland and loves the fact that there is such a huge variety of habitats and species around our shores in close proximity to one another. He has also dived further afield in temperate seas from the Russian White Sea, the cold water coral reefs of Norway, to the sealions, giant octopus and wolf eels of the Canadian Pacific coast. In warmer climes he has carried out surveys in the Red Sea, India, Maldives, Malaysia and the Caribbean.

Chris is a self-taught marine naturalist and this is his second book in this series. He is happiest underwater with a slate in one hand and a camera in the other.

Anemones and corals are found in all marine habitats from rockpools to the edge of the continental shelf and can be the dominant cover over some rocky seabeds. Here are abundant *Actinia equina* in a sea cave in Sark, Channel Islands.

Acknowledgements

Many people contributed to the first edition of this guide through discussions, exchanges of emails and their observations as divers. I would particularly like to thank Bernard Picton of the Ulster Museum, and Richard Manuel, whose Linnaean Society Guide provided me with a mass of useful information and whose early Anthozoan Guide for the (then) Underwater Conservation Society provided much of the stimulus for the first edition. Liz Sides of the National Parks and Wildlife Service in Ireland provided information on conservation measures in Ireland. Bernard Picton (Ulster Museum), Keith Hiscock (Marine Biological Association), Rohan Holt (Countryside Council for Wales) and Sue Daly all read the text in draft and made useful and constructive comments and contributions.

Bernard Picton and Keith Hiscock have also contributed to this second edition, as have many others, including Jason Hall Spencer (University of Plymouth), Charlotte Bolton, Sally Sharrock and Owen Paisley (Seasearch coordinators).

All of the Seasearch guides rely on the skills of underwater photographers to bring them to life. The majority of the images in this second edition are new, as those in the first edition were all from film. Almost all of the photographic contributors are involved in Seasearch in one way or another, whether as tutors, recorders or contributors to our stock of marine life photos for use in Seasearch training and projects. The pictures they have contributed are all marked with their initials, the remaining ones are my own. My many thanks to them all. Bernard Picton (BP), Chris Emblow (CE), Christine Howson (CH), Dan Bolt (DB), Dawn Watson (DW), Erling Svensen (ES), George Brown (GB), Keith Hiscock (KH), Marc Dando (MD), Matt Jeanes (MJ), Mike Markey (MMa), Maura Mitchell (MM), Owen Paisley (OP), Phil Lightfoot (PL), Paul Naylor (PN), Rachel Shucksmith (RJS), Richard Durrant (RD), Rohan Holt (RH), Richard Manuel (RM), Richard Morton (RMo), Rob Spray (RS), Richard Yorke (RY), Sue Daly (SD), Sue Scott (SS), Sally Sharrock (SSh), Steve Trewellha (ST) and Tony Gilbert (TG). Thanks are also due to Sue Daly for her lovely line drawings.

Thanks are also due to the Seasearch supporters who helped with the costs of bringing out the first edition. They were (using their names at the time, some of which have subsequently changed); the Heritage Lottery Fund, English Nature, Countryside Council for Wales, Scottish Natural Heritage, Environment and Heritage Service (Northern Ireland) and the Joint Nature Conservation Committee.

Finally I would like to thank Julie Dando and Marc Dando of Wild Nature Press for all their enthusiasm and design skills which have brought this second edition to fruition.

The scope of this guide

The animals included in this guide fall into the following nine groups:

Soft corals – colonies of tiny polyps with a soft fleshy body
Sea fans – colonies of tiny polyps with a flexible horny skeleton
Sea pens – tall colonies of polyps living partly buried in soft sediment
Stoloniferans – colonies of polyps rising from a thin encrusting membrane
Tube anemones – individual polyps living in a tube, usually buried in soft sediment
Colonial anemones – colonies of polyps with an encrusting common base
Sea anemones – individual polyps, usually attached to a hard surface
Corallimorpharians – individual polyps with a club-like tip to the tentacles
Hard corals – colonies or individual polyps with a hard calcareous skeleton

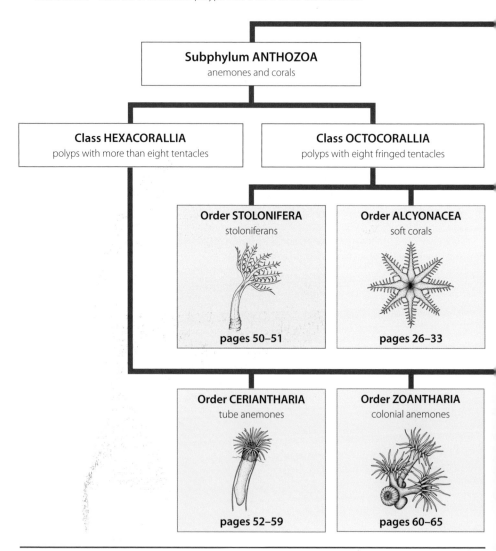

Subphylum ANTHOZOA
anemones and corals

Class HEXACORALLIA
polyps with more than eight tentacles

Class OCTOCORALLIA
polyps with eight fringed tentacles

Order STOLONIFERA
stoloniferans
pages 50–51

Order ALCYONACEA
soft corals
pages 26–33

Order CERIANTHARIA
tube anemones
pages 52–59

Order ZOANTHARIA
colonial anemones
pages 60–65

All of the anemones and corals fall within the Phylum CNIDARIA (pronounced Ny-daria). The name comes from the Latin cnidae meaning nettle and all of the members of the phylum have stinging cells which are used both for the capture of prey and for protection. There are three groups of cnidarians, the ANTHOZOA which are the subject of this guide, the HYDROZOA or hydroids and the SCYPHOZOA or jellyfish.

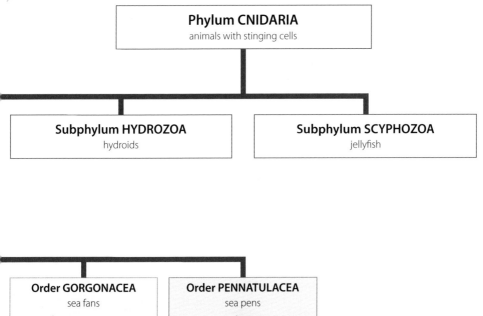

| **Phylum CNIDARIA** |
| animals with stinging cells |

| **Subphylum HYDROZOA** | **Subphylum SCYPHOZOA** |
| hydroids | jellyfish |

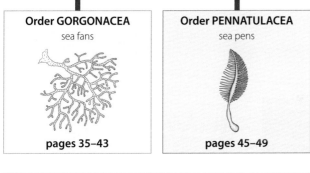

Order GORGONACEA
sea fans

pages 35–43

Order PENNATULACEA
sea pens

pages 45–49

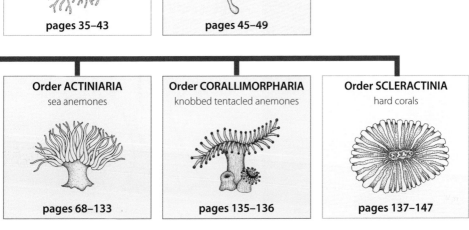

Order ACTINIARIA
sea anemones

pages 68–133

Order CORALLIMORPHARIA
knobbed tentacled anemones

pages 135–136

Order SCLERACTINIA
hard corals

pages 137–147

Structure of the anemone polyp

All of the **Anthozoa** are based on a similar structure, that of the **polyp**. This can be single, as in the case of most of the anemones and the cup corals, or it can be joined with other polyps in a colony, as are the soft corals, sea fans and many of the tropical hard corals.

The anemone or coral polyp has a hollow, cylindrical, body known as the **column**. The lower end may be joined by connecting soft tissues to other polyps in the form of a colony. It may have a basal disc which adheres to hard surfaces and allows some movement by muscular contractions. Alternatively it may be rounded and either burrow directly into soft sediments or live in a tube which itself is buried in sand or mud.

The column may be smooth or may have a series of suckers or **verrucae** either all over it, or just at the upper end. The upper end of the column has a collar in some species, especially the Plumose Anemone, *Metridium dianthus* (formerly *Metridium senile*), which is shown below.

The upper end of the column flattens into an **oral disk** which has a slit-like mouth at its centre and is surrounded by a number of **tentacles**. The tentacles are hollow and either simple, as in the **hexacorals**, or with opposing rows of small offshoots, or **pinnae**, as in the colonial **octocorals**. The upper end of the column is known as the **parapet** and there may be a small valley between it and the tentacles known as the **fosse**.

From the mouth a flattened tube, the **actinopharynx**, leads internally into the body cavity or **coelenteron**. The internal surface of the actinopharynx has one or more longitudinal grooves with tiny hairs, or **cilia**, which can direct a current of water into the body. This is used both for respiration and to inflate or deflate the polyp by changing the hydrostatic pressure. The effect of this is most clearly shown in the Plumose Anemone which can change from being an erect anemone up to 20cm tall to an unattractive deflated blob, by decreasing the internal hydrostatic pressure.

The coelentron is divided up into a series of chambers by radially arranged walls of tissues known as **mesenteries**. These can often be seen as longitudinal lines on the column or as radial lines on the disc. The spaces between the mesenteries are known as **radii** and each one has a single hollow tentacle at its upper end. This means that the cavity inside each tentacle is linked directly with the body cavity. The mesenteries contain the reproductive and digestive processes as well as muscular tissue.

Most of these features are shown below in the photograph and sketch of a small Plumose Anemone *M. dianthus*.

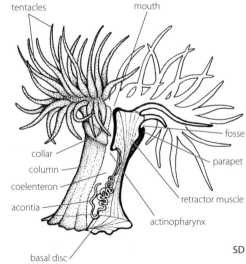

tentacles   mouth

fosse

parapet

collar

column

coelenteron

acontia

retractor muscle

actinopharynx

basal disc

SD

The arrangement of tentacles is one of the features that can be used to distinguish between species. Many species have concentric rings of tentacles with either six or ten in the innermost ring. These primary tentacles are usually the largest and may be held more upright than the remainder. The second ring normally has the same number of tentacles but following rings normally double in number of the last ring but decrease in size.

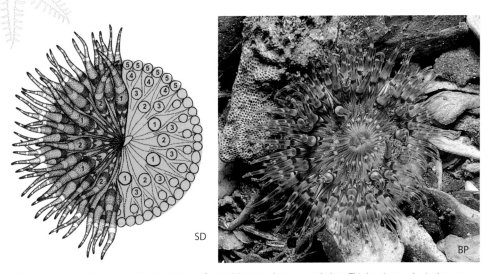

SD

BP

The drawing and picture shows the arrangement for Mud Sagartia, *Sagartia troglodytes*. This has 6 tentacles in the two inner rows, 12 in the third, then 24, 48 and 96 giving a total of 192. However, it is often difficult to make out the rings *in situ* and the situation is complicated by the fact that many anemones are the result of asexual reproduction and are irregular in their layout.

Many anemones are able to contract the tentacles and oral disk into the body cavity for protection and when they are not feeding. The soft corals and sea fans are examples of colonial polyps which are able to contract into the common tissue mass or **coenenchyme**. Other colonial anemones are joined by a much narrower stolon which encrusts rocky and organic surfaces and does not provide any physical strength to the colony. Tube anemones can retract into their tube and many others, notably the Plumose Anemone, commonly retract their mouth and tentacles when there is little passing current. Other anemones do not retract their tentacles, the most common examples being the Snakelocks Anemone, *Anemonia viridis* and Sea Loch Anemone, *Protanthea simplex*.

Snakelocks Anemones *Anemonia viridis* do not retract their tentacles, even when out of the water. Lundy, Devon.

KH

13

Cnidae and feeding

All of the Cnidaria, including all sea anemones and corals, possess stinging cells, or **cnidae**, which are used both for defence and feeding.

The externally-oriented side of the cell has a hair-like trigger called a cnidocil which is activated by touch or chemical stimulus.

There are three main types of cnidae:

Nematocysts are harpoon-like structures. Each one is a microscopic, hollow, capsule which contains an inverted hollow tube that can be ejected with significant force and often pierce the tissues of prey or potential predators. The drawing shows an undischarged nematocyst (top) contained within the cell, and a discharged nematocyst (bottom) showing the penetrative toxic barbs. Nematocysts occur in all of the anthozoa and other Cnidaria and are found in most tissues, including the tentacles.

Spirocysts are lasso-like strings that are fired at prey and wrap around a cellular projection on the prey. They are unique to Hexacorallia where they occur mostly in the tentacles.

Ptychocysts have a sticky surface used to stick to prey, and in burrowing (tube) anemones, help to create the tube in which the animal lives.

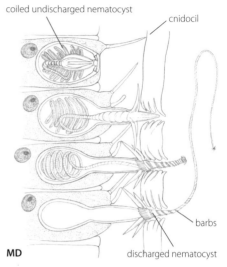

coiled undischarged nematocyst

cnidocil

barbs

MD

discharged nematocyst

From top to bottom this sequence shows the stimulated cnidocil triggering the discharge of the coiled nematocyst.

SS

The anemone on the left is using its acontia to possibly deter another encroaching hermit crab, also with an anemone attached.

Many of the cnidae possess toxins which can stun prey or sting predators. These toxins are best known to us in many species of jellyfish where the level of toxin is high enough to be felt by humans. We can also see cnidae in action by touching the tentacles of a Snakelocks Anemone, *Anemonia viridis* or Beadlet Anemone, *Actinia equina* and feeling the way the tentacles stick to our fingers as the cnidae are discharged.

Each cnida can only be discharged once and new cnidae are produced within the animal to replace those discharged. This process uses a lot of energy and chemosensors allow only the right combination of stimuli to cause discharge. This prevents the animal from stinging itself. The immature cnidae are known as cnidoblasts.

Some species produce nematocysts on long threads known as **acontia**. These are attached internally and can be used to subdue active prey which has been ingested. However the free ends can be extended out of the mouth and also used to deter predators. The species in which this is most often seen are the two anemones that live with hermit crabs, Parasitic Anemone, *Calliactis parasitica* and Cloak Anemone, *Adamsia palliata*.

Acontia may be visible internally through the column. There is a picture of a Jewel Anemone on page 136, in which the acontia can be clearly seen.

Some acontinate anemones have **catch tentacles**. These are modified inner tentacles with many nematocysts which can be used in aggressive behaviour towards other anemones and potential predators.

Catch tentacle of Plumose Anemone, *Metridium dianthus*. Isle of Man.

Another variation with an aggressive function is the presence of **acrorhagi** in some species. These are hollow warts which contain numerous nematocysts. The form a single encircling rim around the top of the column and are most obvious in Beadlet Anemones, *Actinia equina* (see picture on p. 89). These can be used to deter other anemones, which may be important where the density is high.

Whilst the food of most anemones consists of small organisms, a number of the larger species can be seen taking much larger prey. Dahlia Anemones, *Urticina felina*, in particular are seen ingesting a variety of species. Some examples of feeding behaviour are shown in the following pictures.

The rare anemone *Arachnanthus sarsi* using a tentacle to pass a small shrimp into its mouth. Rathlin Island, Northern Ireland.

Beadlet Anemone, *Actinia equina*, ingesting a surprisingly large jellyfish. Sark, Channel Islands.

Dahlia Anemone, *Urticina felina*, eating a crab. It is not clear whether such a large prey item has been caught alive or if it has fallen into the anemone's span of tentacles after death. Anglesey.

Anemones do not have it all their own way, however, as they in turn can be predated upon by starfish, nudibranchs and other mobile feeders. Some nudibranchs are obligate feeders on soft corals and anemones – see pages 66–67 for more information.

Red Cushion Star, *Porania pulvillus*, in the process of feeding on a Dead Men's Finger, *Alcyonium digitatum*.

Reproduction

Sea anemones and corals reproduce both sexually and asexually and some are able to do both. In sexual reproduction fertilisation may take place either internally or externally. External fertilisation takes places following the ejection of eggs and sperm into the water from one anemone, or, in the case of sea fans, release of eggs from beneath the surface tissue (image p. 37). Release into the water is rarely observed by divers but can be seen in the image of the Imperial Anemone *Capnea sanguinea* below.

Internal fertilisation can involve a period of brooding and the subsequent release of fully formed young anemones. This is known as **viviparity** and is most commonly observed in Beadlet Anemones *Actinia equina* and Daisy Anemones *Cereus pedunculatus*.

Spawning Imperial Anemone, *Capnea sanguinea*, Kilkieran Bay, Galway.

Daisy Anemone, *Cereus pedunculatus*, in the process of ejecting fully formed live young from its mouth. Loch Carron, Highland.

New colonial anemones and corals develop from a single larva which, after a short free-swimming period, settles on a suitable surface and develops into a single ancestral polyp. Once established, the single polyp can reproduce asexually, normally by budding (see below) and thus gradually build up a new colony.

Asexual reproduction takes place in all of the groups of sea anemones and corals except for the tube anemones (Ceriantharia). It occurs in four main ways:

Budding takes place in all of the colonial forms. In the case of the soft corals, sea fans, colonial anemones and colonial corals new polyps bud from the connecting tissue between existing polyps or even from the walls of existing polyps.

KH

A complex arrangement of polyps on a Pink Sea Fan, *Eunicella verrucosa*, as a result of budding. Plymouth, Devon.

Longitudinal fission takes place in Jewel Anemones *Corynactis viridis* and some of the Actiniaria (sea anemones) and in a modified form some of the hard corals. Here an existing anemone stretches itself by elongating its base and then splits in two across the middle, resulting in two new anemones of the same size. This process happens over a few hours, but is very rarely observed in the wild. The image shows two jewel anemones which appear to be in the final stages of breaking apart with only the mouth parts remaining fused together.

18 SEA ANEMONES AND CORALS

This method of reproduction is the reason that Jewel Anemones often occur in patches, each with a different colour. Jewel Anemones like many others, have a variety of colour forms but those forming a patch of one colour are likely to be all produced from one original anemone by a series of longitudinal fission processes.

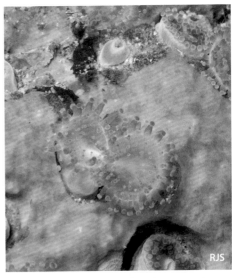

Patches of Jewel Anemones, *Corynactis viridis*, carpet a rock wall. Sark, Channel Islands.

Jewel Anemones, *Corynactis viridis*, in the process of longitudinal fission. Shetland.

Divers have also reported Dahlia Anemones *Urticina felina* in the process of splitting, This anemone is thought to normally reproduce sexually and, whilst asexual reproduction by longitudinal fission has been recorded it is unlikely to be common as this species, unlike the Jewel Anemone, does not have a tendency for similar colour forms to cluster closely together. The photograph shows a splitting Dahlia Anemone having reached the stage where there are separate mouths but not all of the two rings of tentacles have been produced.

Dahlia Anemone, *Urticina felina* in the process of longitudinal fission. Loch Carron, Highland.

Transverse fission is much less common and occurs where an anemone splits lengthways. In the case of two species, Trumpet Anemone *Aiptasia couchii* and Starlet Sea Anemone *Nematostella vectensis*, the anemone develops a constriction on the lower part of the column, which is eventually pinched off. The upper part grows a new base, whilst the lower part remains attached and generates a new disk, mouth and tentacles. *Gonactinia prolifera* grows a new ring of tentacles around the column before the anemones separate. This can be seen occurring in the picture of this anemone on page 70. Finally the Wedge Coral, *Sphenotrochus andrewianus*, which is free living, develops new disk, tentacles and mouth at the basal end and then separates in the middle.

Basal laceration occurs where small fragments of tissue separate from the lower part of the column just above the base. These then develop into tiny anemones. One common anemone that does this is the Elegant Anemone *Sagartia elegans* and is the reason why different colour varieties commonly cluster together. Another is the Plumose Anemone *Metridium dianthus* where there are commonly a number of small anemones clustered around the base of an adult which have all split off from it. This can be seen in the photograph.

Small Plumose Anemones, *Metridium dianthus*, clustering around the base of the 'parent' as a result of basal laceration. Lands End, Cornwall.

The method of reproduction is one of the complicating factors in anemone identification. Those species which commonly reproduce by longitudinal fission or basal laceration often end up being irregular and losing the characteristic numbers and arrangement of rings of tentacles. One of the obvious signs of irregularity is the mouth which becomes three or more sided rather than a simple slit, as in the picture to the right.

Three sided mouth in an Elegant Anemone, *Sagartia elegans*. Hand Deeps, Devon.

English names

The great majority of anemones were given English names by Gosse (1860). Many of them have survived, such as Plumose Anemone and Daisy Anemone, even though the generic name has changed. Others have slightly changed. What we now call the Snakelocks Anemone was originally Snake-locked Anemone. Other names have never really come into common use, such as Glaucus Pimplet and Warted Corklet. Some of the original names have been omitted intentionally as they are misleading. For example Gosse called *Sagartia troglodytes* the Cave-dwelling Anemone as its specific name suggests. However, we now know that these anemones are usually found in open sand and gravelly areas and not in caves. This species appears here as Mud Sagartia which is a more recent name and better reflects the habitat in which it is found. A few other names are recent, such as Elegant Anemone for *Sagartia elegans*. Originally the colour varieties of this anemone were thought to be a different species so Gosse does not have a name for the united species we now recognise. Most of Gosse's names end with the -let suffix denoting small.

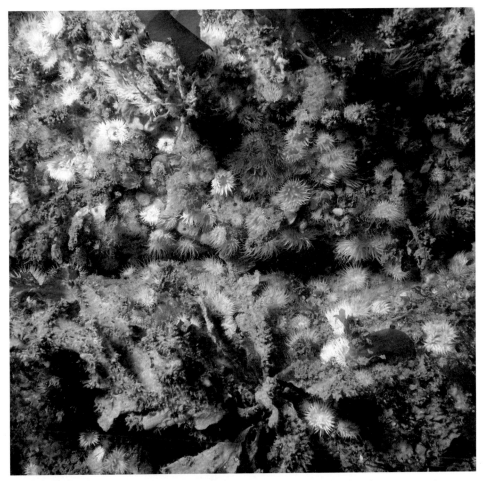

Three colour varieties of Elegant Anemone, *Sagartia elegans*. These were originally thought to be separate species. Eddystone, Devon.

Some common confusions

Members of other groups of marine animals can occasionally look like anemones and corals and this is not helped by some English names such as Ross or Rose Coral (which is a bryozoan) and Coral Weed (a seaweed). Here are some common confusions.

Jellyfish

The Moon Jellyfish, *Aurelia aurita*, has an unusual lifecycle which includes a period when it is attached to rocky surfaces and closely resembles a stoloniferan. Following a brief swimming period, new planulae larvae attach to a hard surface and develop into tiny sessile animals known as scyphistomae. These reproduce by asexual budding and eventually release free-swimming tiny immature jellyfish. Whilst attached to the rock there are commonly huge numbers of the tiny scyphistomae giving a white fluffy appearance. They are usually found in shallow water and underneath overhanging surfaces.

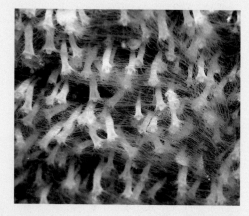

Hydroids

Hydroids are in the same phylum as Anthozoans and in some species the polyp-like hydranths are large enough to look like tiny anemones. The common Oaten Pipe Hydroid, *Tubularia indivisa* (below), and Nodding Hydroid, *Corymorpha nutans*, are two examples. Some of the taller hydroids, such as the Antenna Hydroid, *Nemertesia antennina* (left), can be confused with sea pens but can be easily distinguished on habitat grounds alone as hydroids will be attached to a hard surface, whereas sea pens burrow into soft sediments.

Worms

Annelid worms which live in tubes often have a brachial crown or fan which looks like the tentacles of an anemone. They do not contain nematocysts but are used to assist respiration and as passive receptacles for food particles falling from the water column. Two different worms are shown in the photograph, left Eyelash Worm *Myxicola infundibulum* and right *Megalomma vesiculosum*. A useful tip for distinguishing worms from anemones underwater is that the worms are much more likely to retract instantly into their tubes whereas anemones generally contract more slowly.

Sponges

Erect branching sponges can superficially look like sea fans but do not possess polyps, or a hard skeleton. Photograph shows Yellow Staghorn Sponge, *Axinella dissimilis* (right) next to Red Sea Fingers, *Alcyonium glomeratum*.

Sea cucumbers

Borrowing or crevice-dwelling sea cucumbers have feeding tentacles which are commonly the only part of the animal that is visible. These tentacles are usually branched as opposed to anemone tentacles which are undivided which can be seen clearly on this Gravel Sea Cucumber, *Neopentadactyla mixta*.

How to use this guide

In the descriptions of individual species that follow the standard taxonomic classification has been generally followed. All of the species in the MCS/Ulster Museum Species Directory listed as occurring in Britain and Ireland are referred to, though some rare or deepwater species do not have full descriptions. However, since the publication of the Species Directory a number of names have been changed and these have been updated in this second edition to follow species names accepted in WoRMS, the World Register of Marine Species, at the time of writing. There is a taxonomically ordered list of species on pages 157–158.

Where the standard taxonomic order has been departed from is in the largest group, the Actiniaria, which includes most of the sea anemones. Here there are so many species that they have been grouped by habitat and behaviour so that similar species are close together.

The species descriptions are therefore ordered as follows:

Soft corals	Octocorallia, Order Alcyonacea	pages 26–33
Sea fans	Octocorallia, Order Gorgonacea	pages 35–43
Sea pens	Octocorallia, Order Pennatulacea	pages 45–49
Stoloniferans	Octocorallia, Order Stolonifera	pages 50–51
Tube anemones	Hexacorallia, Order Ceriantharia	pages 52–59
Colonial anemones	Hexacorallia, Order Zoantharia	pages 60–65
Sea anemones	Hexacorallia, Order Actiniaria	pages 68–133
Sea anemones that usually occur in **groups or aggregations**, and related spp.		pages 69–87
Sea anemones that live on the **shore or in shallow water**		pages 88–111
Sea anemones that live on **soft seabeds**		pages 112–124
Sea anemones that live on **other animals**		pages 125–134
Coralliomorpharians	Hexacorallia, Order Corallimorpharia	pages 135–136
Hard corals	Hexacorallia, Order Scleractinia	pages 137–147

For each species the following information is given, where known:

GENERAL DESCRIPTION

KEY FEATURES The main identifying features for the species.

SIMILAR TO Other anemones or corals with which the species could be confused and how to distinguish them.

DISTRIBUTION the map shows the known distribution in Britain and Ireland taken from Seasearch records, the National Biodiversity Network and other sources. For each area the abundance is shown as:

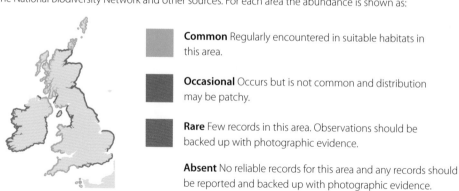

Common Regularly encountered in suitable habitats in this area.

Occasional Occurs but is not common and distribution may be patchy.

Rare Few records in this area. Observations should be backed up with photographic evidence.

Absent No reliable records for this area and any records should be reported and backed up with photographic evidence.

SIZE A guide, using parts of the body, to the size of an individual anemone or coral, or, in the case of colonial forms, the size of a typical colony.

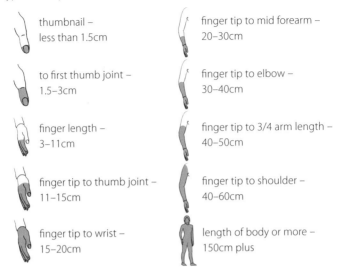

thumbnail –
less than 1.5cm

to first thumb joint –
1.5–3cm

finger length –
3–11cm

finger tip to thumb joint –
11–15cm

finger tip to wrist –
15–20cm

finger tip to mid forearm –
20–30cm

finger tip to elbow –
30–40cm

finger tip to 3/4 arm length –
40–50cm

finger tip to shoulder –
40–60cm

length of body or more –
150cm plus

HABITAT This shows the habitats in which each species can be found. **Rock** includes reefs, boulders and stone. **Sand** includes coarse sand and gravel. **On other animals and plants** denotes that the species is usually found on specific other animals, on seaweeds or living on shells, both alive and dead.

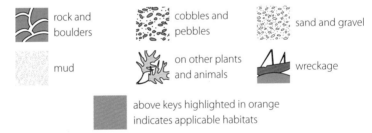

rock and
boulders

cobbles and
pebbles

sand and gravel

mud

on other plants
and animals

wreckage

above keys highlighted in orange
indicates applicable habitats

DEPTH Shore includes both the lower shore and rockpools and shallow sublittoral habitats down to about 10m depth, **Mid** depth is from 10m to 25m depth and **Deep** is below 25m.

lower shore and
shallow water 0–10m

mid depth 10–25m

deep water more
than 25m

CONSERVATION STATUS

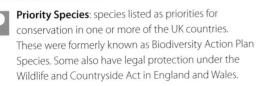

Priority Species: species listed as priorities for conservation in one or more of the UK countries. These were formerly known as Biodiversity Action Plan Species. Some also have legal protection under the Wildlife and Countryside Act in England and Wales.

Non-native: species which have arrived from elsewhere in the recent past.

Soft corals
Octocorallia, Order Alcyonacea

Soft corals are colonial animals that form either encrusting sheets or erect fleshy masses, often with finger-like branches. The surface is covered in large numbers of individual polyps. The polyp has eight tentacles, each of which has two rows of tiny offshoots along it. These are known as pinnate tentacles. The body is strengthened by the presence of tiny calcareous splinters within it called sclerites.

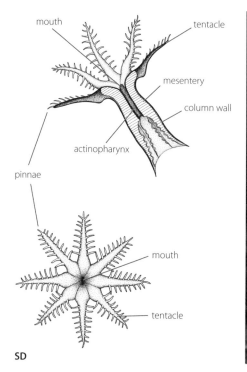

SD

Photo and drawings of polyps of Red Sea Fingers, *Alcyonium glomeratum*.

Soft corals are usually attached to rocky surfaces though they may occur on other stable surfaces such as cobbles and large shells.

New soft coral colonies arise from the dispersal of free-swimming larvae. The length of time these can survive in the plankton determines how easily the species can spread and colonise new surfaces. A tiny proportion of the larvae settle and develop into an ancestral polyp which then creates a colony by asexual budding. New polyps bud from tubular connections between existing polyps or directly from the walls of the polyps themselves.

Soft corals have a worldwide distribution and are found at all depths from the lower shore to at least 9,000m. However, there are only three species in shallow British and Irish waters, one of which, Dead Men's Fingers *Alcyonium digitatum* is very common.

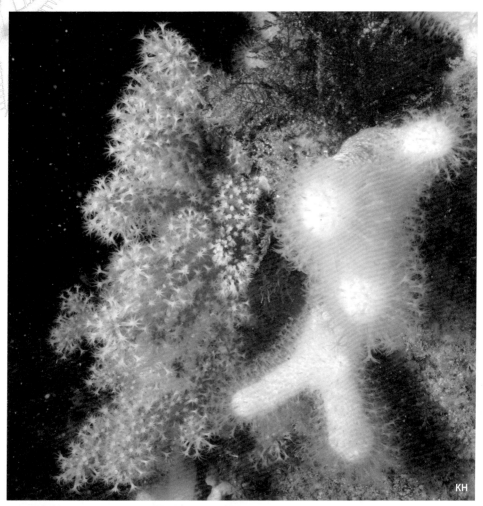

Dead Men's Fingers, *Alcyonium digitatum* and Red Sea Fingers, *Alcyonium glomeratum* can be found together in southwest England. Blackstone Point, Devon.

Pink Soft Coral, *Alcyonium hibernicum*, in close up showing larvae brooding in the polyps.

Alcyonium digitatum Dead Men's Fingers

Orange and white colour forms of *Alcyonium digitatum* with extended and contracted polyps. St Abbs, Borders.

This common colonial soft coral has an orange, yellow or white body with blunt, finger-like projections up to 25cm tall. The polyps are found all over the body. They are translucent white in colour and closely spaced giving a furry outline when they are extended to feed. When not feeding the smooth and rather bloated looking fingers show how the common name arose.

Alcyonium digitatum are found on rocks and boulders, and occasionally on cobbles and shells, from the lower shore down to about 50m. They are also very common on steel wrecks.

As filter feeders they prefer areas with some current and can withstand turbulent conditions. Places where they are particularly common are on North Sea coasts around St Abbs and the Farne Islands, in current-swept channels in the Isle of Man and in the entrance to sea lochs in western Scotland. Here you can often see them mixed with brittlestars. They occur on wrecks throughout Britain and Ireland.

The different colour forms are found together in many places and there does not seem to be any regional or habitat difference between them. White forms may be a little more common in the south and most colonies on the west coast of Ireland are orange.

Alcyonium digitatum often cover shipwrecks such as this fishing vessel in the Moray Firth.

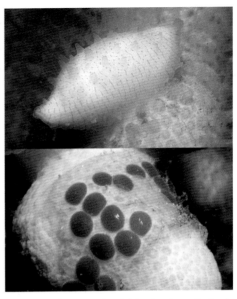

Tritonia hombergi eating *Alcyonium digitatum*. Loch Carron, Highland.

False Cowrie, *Simnia patula*, adult (top) and eggs (bottom). The Lizard, Cornwall.

Two molluscs commonly live and feed on Dead Men's Fingers. These are the large sea-slug *Tritonia hombergi*, particularly in Scottish waters, and the False Cowrie, *Simnia patula*, most often seen in Devon and Cornwall.

A. digitatum have a dormant period over the autumn and winter when the polyps are permanently retracted and the whole colony may become discoloured and covered in filamentous red algae and other material. The covering material will be expelled in the early spring when the colonies spawn and begin to feed again.

A. digitatum are long-living and can survive for over 25 years.

KEY FEATURES White or orange colonies often covering large areas.

SIMILAR TO Easily distinguished from other soft corals by size, colour and density of polyps. It is important to recognise them with and without the polyps extended.

Dormant colony with algal cover. Isle of Man.

Alcyonium glomeratum Red Sea Fingers

SD

Expanded colony. Sark, Channel Islands.

This colonial soft coral has a deep red body with slim 'fingers' growing up to 20cm tall. The polyps are spread all over the body and are translucent white, contrasting with the red body colour. When the polyps are retracted the body has a warty texture and can look rather deflated.

Alcyonium glomeratum are found on steep or overhanging rock surfaces, usually out of, but close to, areas of strong water movement. In some cases, especially in the south, where they can be more common than *Alcyonium digitatum*, they may cover large areas.

Elsewhere, usually towards the edge of the distribution range, there are colonies with the widely spaced polyps characteristic of this species, but a white or pale yellow body colour reminiscent of *A. digitatum*. The taxonomic status of this form is uncertain.

KEY FEATURES Prominent white polyps on red body.
SIMILAR TO *A. digitatum* (p. 28) but slimmer red fingers and more prominent polyps.

Contracted colony. Hilsea Point, Devon.

Close up of *Alcyonium glomeratum* polyps clearly showing the eight fringed tentacles on each one. Hand Deeps, Cornwall.

Pale yellow species intermediate between *Alcyonium glomeratum* and *Alcyonium digitatum*. Donegal.

Alcyonium hibernicum Pink Soft Coral

A small colony of *Alcyonium hibernicum* amongst *Alcyonium digitatum*, South Uist, Hebrides.

This tiny soft coral, also known as Pink Sea Fingers, grows either as small fingers up to 4cm tall or as a thin encrustation with the polyps on slightly raised nodules with a clear area between them. Specimens from Britain and Ireland are mostly pink with a white rim below the tentacles of the polyps giving a slightly spangled appearance.

Alcyonium hibernicum is nearly always found under overhangs or in caves, well out of the light and sheltered from water movements.

The taxonomy has been recently revised by McFadden (1999). The name *Parerythropodium* or *Alcyonium coralloides* has been used in the past but this is now thought to be a more southerly species. *A. hibernicum* has been identified as a separate species based on specimens from the Isle of Man and Ireland.

This is a scarce species and not often recorded, though there is anecdotal evidence that numbers are increasing in some southerly locations.

The patchy distribution compared to the other soft corals suggests that the larvae do not survive long in the plankton, thus limiting the spread of the species.

Partly contracted colony. Isle of Man.

KEY FEATURES Small pink colonies in shaded places
SIMILAR TO Small *Alcyonium digitatum* (p. 28) or Stoloniferans (p. 50) which also have eight fringed tentacles on each polyp. The colour should help distinguish them.

The Sugar Loaf Caves on the Isle of Man are a well-known location for this species.

Alcyopnium hibernicum – red colour morph

The image below is of a small soft coral that comes from a shallow surge gully in the Isles of Scilly. Though it looks quite different to Pink Soft Coral, both in colour and morphology, McFadden suggests it is more likely to be a colour morph of *A. hibernicum* rather than the more southerly *A. coralloides*. More records of this form would be valuable and are most likely to come from the Channel Islands or south-western Ireland. It occurs in French waters in the Isles Chausey south of Jersey.

SD

A large, healthy Pink Sea Fan, *Eunicella verrucosa*. Sark, Channel Islands.

Sea fans
Octocorallia, Order Gorgonacea

The sea fans, like the soft corals, are octocorals and their polyps have eight fringed tentacles. The colonies are branching and each branch is a rod-like structure which is calcified and strengthened with internal bone-like fragments known as **sclerites**. The colonies usually branch in one plane and are commonly aligned at right angles to the prevailing water current so that each polyp benefits equally from passing food. The colony as a whole is flexible enough to withstand water movement, though it does not tolerate strong turbulence, and is easily snapped off by physical contact.

Polyps occur all along the branches in an irregular fashion though they are mostly aligned along the plane of the colony as a whole. They can be retracted into the skeleton.

Sea fans are usually attached to rocks though they may attach to other stable surfaces such as wrecks and boulders.

Sea fan colonies grow by the process of asexual budding. New polyps bud from tubular connections between existing polyps or directly from the walls of the polyps themselves. New colonies are formed by the settlement of planulae larvae from the zooplankton. The larva grows into a single polyp but by the time the colony is 1cm tall it will have three or four. Studies of the Pink Sea Fan, *Eunicella verrucosa*, in south Devon have shown that young colonies may grow by 6–7cm per year whilst established ones grow much more slowly, only about 1cm.

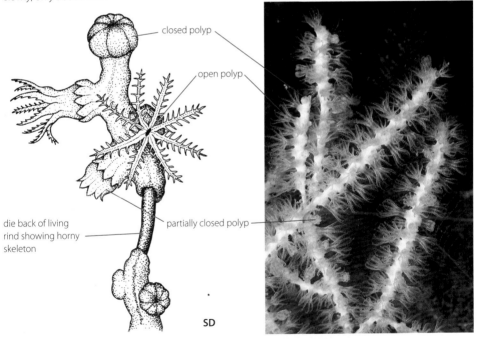

closed polyp

open polyp

die back of living
rind showing horny
skeleton

partially closed polyp

SD

Sea fans have a worldwide distribution and there are many species, some of which grow to 3m across. There are only two species in British and Irish waters though 20 have been recorded from the European Atlantic coasts and the Mediterranean. These include Precious Coral, *Corallium rubrum*, the source of red coral jewellery.

Eunicella verrucosa Pink Sea Fan

Part of a sea fan 'forest'. Plymouth, Devon.

Eunicella verrucosa has a distinctive, many-branched, growth form and normally forms a distinctive fan shape with all of the branches in a single plane. The usual size of fully grown colonies is about 30cm tall and 40cm wide but Seasearch diver surveys have recorded them up to 75cm across in the Channel Islands. Pink Sea Fans are commonly found on open rocky surfaces at depths of 20m or more where there is little turbulence but may occur shallower in some sheltered conditions such as inside the breakwater at Plymouth. Occasionally colonies are bushy rather than fan shaped. This is where local currents are either very weak or multi-directional.

A large sea fan in good condition. Manacles, Cornwall.

White and pink *Eunicella verrucosa* together. Bigbury Bay, Devon.

A sea fan brooding eggs beneath the outer tissue seen in July at the Manacles, Cornwall.

In some areas very large numbers of *E. verrucosa* grow close together in a 'forest' with up to 20 fans per square metre. This usually occurs on deeper flat bedrock or on the flattened plates of wrecks.

New colonies are formed by larval dispersal and initially are in the form of single stems. They may grow up to 10cm in the first year but they then begin to branch and the growth rate slows to as little as 1cm per annum. Large colonies may be over 50 years old.

First-year sea fan recruits. Sark, Channel Islands.

Sea fan nudibranch (left) and its eggs (right). Devon.

Despite its name the colour is variable from white to yellow to an orangey-pink. The pink form is the most common in British waters though occasional white or buff colonies occur. However *E. verrucosa* is often white in southern Ireland and at some sites both colours occur. In southern Europe and the Mediterranean they are all white.

Since the sea fan is usually aligned across currents it can become fouled by drifting organisms such as seaweeds. Catsharks often use them to attach their egg cases, or Mermaid's Purses, to and some animals, such as barnacles and bryozoans, settle on them. There is even an anemone which lives exclusively on sea fans and other rod-like animals (see *Amphianthus dohrnii* on p. 129). When colonies die they often remain attached to the seabed and become covered by a wide range of fouling organisms. The upright form and its orientation across currents provides an attractive habitat for other filter feeders.

There are few animals that actually prey on *E. verrucosa*, most are repulsed by the stinging nematocysts in the tentacles. However nudibranchs or sea slugs have adapted to feed on various anemones and corals

False Cowrie, *Simnia hiscocki*. South Devon.

as well as many other animals. The sea slug that is found on the sea fan is *Tritonia nilsodhneri*, which is well camouflaged to look like the sea fan itself. *Tritonia* lays its characteristic spirals of eggs around sea fan branches. The False Cowrie, *Simnia hiscocki* (a close relative to the species that occurs on Dead Men's Fingers, *Alcyonium digitatum* – see p. 28) can also be found seen feeding on *E. verrucosa*.

E. verrucosa has a limited distribution in Britain and Ireland. Seasearch is particularly interested to hear about any extensions in the range, and records from North Donegal, North Wales, the Isle of Man or East Dorset would be particularly valuable. Outside Britain and Ireland it also occurs throughout the north-east Atlantic, south to north Africa and in the Mediterranean.

Whilst *E. verrucosa* does not provide a suitable material for coral jewellery it has been collected in the past to be dried as a decoration, and much damage has been done by fishing gear. Since 1992 it has been a protected species in England and Wales under the Wildlife and Countryside Act (1981). This means it is an offence to kill, injure or take *E. verrucosa* or to be in possession of a live or dead animal or offer it for sale. Awareness of the species amongst fishermen is being increased to minimise damage from trawling, and divers should be particularly careful of not breaking a sea fan when underwater. A careless kick with a fin could kill a fan which might be up to 50 years old.

KEY FEATURES Pink or occasionally white colonies usually in a flattened, fan shape.

SIMILAR TO Sometimes confused with branching sponges by inexperienced observers. The presence of polyps should distinguish it. The Northern Sea Fan, *Swiftia pallida* (p. 42), has a much less regular, straggly growth form and is always white. There is almost no overlap in distribution.

Dead *Eunicella verrucosa* providing a habitat for Jewel Anemones *Corynactis virids*, Dead Men's Fingers *Alcyonium digitatum*, bryozoans and red seaweeds. Sark, Channel Islands.

Pink Sea Fan disease at Lundy and in Bigbury Bay

Pink Sea Fans, *Eunicella verrucosa,* at Lundy have been studied by Marine Conservation Society divers from 1997 to 2002 and by Seasearch since 2003. In Bigbury Bay Seasearch sea fan surveys were undertaken in 2003 and 2005 and there have been incidental records since that time.

It became clear in 2001–2 that there were numbers of dead or dying pink sea fans in the population at Lundy, and that a similar situation was occurring in Bigbury Bay. Hall-Spencer *et al.* recorded diseased sea fans at 7 out of 13 sites in south-west England, including Lundy, and found from video transects that 9% of sea fans showed signs of necrosis.

Left: Pink Sea Fan at Lundy with dead centre and growing extremities.

Opposite page: Dead *Eunicella verrucosa* providing a habitat for hydroids and White-striped Anemones *Actinothoe sphyrodeta.* Sark, Channel Islands.

The disease took the form of 'die back' of the living tissue on mature colonies leading first to a spindly 'wasted' appearance, then to complete loss of tissue exposing the horny skeleton. This was followed by rapid colonisation of the skeleton by a range of fouling organisms and death of many colonies.

Hall-Spencer *et al.* investigated the cause of the necrosis and found significantly higher concentrations of bacteria in diseased specimens than in healthy ones. Of 21 distinct bacteria isolated from diseased tissues, 19 were Vibrionaceae, 15 were strains of *Vibrio splendidus* and 2 others closely matched *Vibrio tasmaniensis.* Vibrios inoculated into healthy sea fans did not result in necrosis at 15°C, but, at 20°C sea fans inoculated with vibros became diseased whilst those not inoculated remained healthy.

Seasearch divers recorded the condition of individual sea fan colonies throughout the range using a simple 5-point scale in which 5 represented a completely healthy colony without any visible damage or fouling and 0 a completely dead and fouled colony. Comparison of the average condition of sea fans at Lundy with other populations in both 2001–2 and 2004–6 showed that the Lundy population was significantly the poorest with condition scores of 2.16 (2001–2) and 3.0 (2004–6) compared to 4.1 (2001–2) and 3.9 (2004–6). Resurvey of two of the sites at Lundy in 2012 gave an average condition score of 3.05, very little changed since 2004–6.

Whilst all of the sites surveyed at Lundy showed low condition scores, in Bigbury Bay the situation was very mixed with some sites diseased and others apparently unaffected. Hall-Spencer *et al.* also found the incidence of necrosis to vary from site to site.

The continuing low scores do not necessarily mean that significant levels of necrosis are still taking place in either location. In Lundy in particular, sea fans can be seen with dead central areas and healthy peripheral

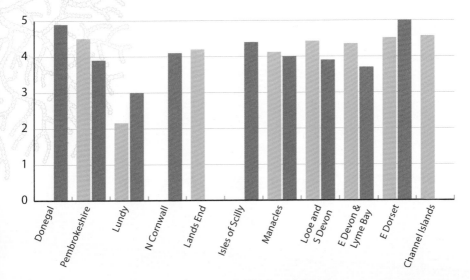

Average sea fan condition scores from Seasearch surveys in ● 2001–2 and ● 2004–6.

growth, and dead colonies can remain attached to the rock surface for many years. Both of these mean that the condition scores will only improve gradually and are dependent on new recruits within the population. Sadly in the Seasearch studies in 2012 at Lundy only 1 out of 152 colonies measured was a single-stemmed specimen and thus the rate of new recruitment to the population is extremely slow.

Hall-Spencer *et al.* found that necrosis increased with higher temperatures, and did not occur in depths in excess of 50m (where temperatures would be lower). This suggests that with increasing sea temperatures more outbreaks of sea fan disease can be expected in the future.

References

Seasearch Pink Sea Fan Surveys 2001–2002.
Chris Wood. Marine Conservation Society. 2003.
– available online at www.seasearch.org.uk

Seasearch Pink Sea Fan Surveys 2004–2006.
Chris Wood. Marine Conservation Society. 2007.
– available online at www.seasearch.org.uk

Diseases affect cold-water corals too: *Eunicella verrucosa* **(Cnidaria: Gorgonacea) necrosis in SW England.** Jason M. Hall-Spencer, James Pike and Colin B. Munn. 2007. *Diseases of Aquatic Organisms.* Vol. 76: 87–97.

Swiftia pallida Northern Sea Fan

A whole colony. Firth of Lorn, Argyll & Bute.

Swiftia pallida has relatively few branches which are arranged in an irregular fashion. It is much more straggly in appearance than *Eunicella verrucosa*. British specimens are white or pale grey in colour, though red or pink forms of the same species occur in the Mediterranean.

S. *pallida* is found on flat and sloping rock surfaces and occasionally on boulders, usually below 20m.

In shallow waters the distribution of this species is limited to the west coast of Scotland and the Kenmare River in south-west Ireland. This apparently strange distribution is because of deep cold water upwellings. S. *pallida* also occurs in deep waters offshore in Ireland, the Bay of Biscay and the Mediterranean, where it occurs as deep as 600m.

KEY FEATURES A white, straggly sea fan, only likely to be seen in Scotland.
SIMILAR TO Easily distinguished from *Eunicella verrucosa* (p. 36) by colony form, colour and distribution.

Swiftia pallida amongst a mixed animal turf containing cup corals, soft corals, hydroids, bryozoans and sponges. Firth of Lorn, Argyll.

Diver with Tall Sea Pen, *Funiculina quadrangularis*. Loch Sunart, Highland.

Sea pens
Octocorallia, Order Pennatulacea

Sea pens, like the soft corals and sea fans, are octocorals and their polyps have eight fringed tentacles. They are unique in that they are the only group of octocorals that live exclusively on muddy or sandy sea-beds. Each colony has a central stalk, the lower part of which is free of polyps and functions as a burrowing organ. This is the part of the sea pen which is buried in the soft sediment. The upper part of the stalk is known as the rachis and bears the polyps either directly on the stalk itself or on pairs of branches.

Most sea pens are capable of luminescence during darkness. This can occur either as isolated flashes or rhythmic pulses of light passing along the whole colony.

There are three British species of sea pens, one of which is widespread. The most likely places they will be encountered by divers is in muddy bottoms of Scottish sea lochs.

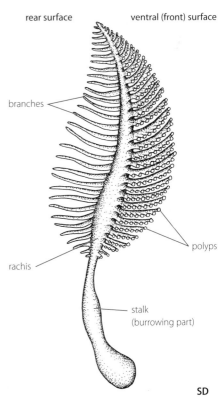

rear surface ventral (front) surface

branches

polyps

rachis

stalk
(burrowing part)

SD

All three species can occur together as here off Oban in 30m.

Funiculina quadrangularis Tall Sea Pen

TG

Loch Nevis, Highland.

The largest of the British and Irish sea pens and can be up to 2m in length. The polyps are distributed along the stalk and the colony is not branched. About a fifth of the colony is buried in the mud. The long colonies have a distinctive curved shape, rather reminiscent of the sea whips of tropical waters. The colour of the colony is white, yellowish or pale pink.

The stalk has a square cross-section which has given the animal its specific name *quadrangularis*.

Funiculina quadrangularis has a very wide distribution and may be found worldwide. Diver records all come from sea lochs along the west coast of Scotland, in depths of 30m or more. Here it is often found with the Norway Lobster or Scampi, *Nephrops norvegicus*. The deepwater brittlestar *Asteronyx loveni* is known to cling to *F. quadrangularis*.

It has been suggested that this sea pen was formerly much more common and that populations have been severely reduced by the effects of Scampi trawling. The dead remains can sometimes be seen dumped in fishing ports where nets and trawls are cleaned. *F. quadrangularis* cannot retract

into the sediment, though they can pull themselves upright again after gentle disturbance.

The colonies (which are of separate sexes) are believed to have a pattern of patchy recruitment, slow growth and have a long lifespan. This makes a population less able to recover from damage than other species. Because of the threats it is a Priority Species.

KEY FEATURES A very tall unbranched colony, in mud.
SIMILAR TO Size and habitat should distinguish this species from anything else. Slender Sea Pen *Virgularia mirabilis* (p. 47) is much smaller.

Funiculina quadrangularis is easily disturbed and colonies can be seen at all angles or even crossing over each other as here in Loch Duich, Highland.

Virgularia mirabilis Slender Sea Pen

Virgularia mirabilis is the sea pen most likely to be encountered by divers in British and Irish waters. It is up to 60cm tall and about half of the total length is buried in the sand and mud in which it lives. It has a mucus-lined burrow into which the whole colony can withdraw quite quickly if disturbed.

The central stalk is straight and round in cross-section. The polyps are on paired branches and there is frequently a bare length of the central stalk at the top of the colony. The length of the side branches tapers towards the top and bottom of the colony producing a delicate profile. Colour is white to yellow and this species is able to luminesce in darkness.

Like the other sea pens, *V. mirabilis* is found on deep muddy bottoms but it can also be found in shallower sheltered waters, and thus frequently occurs in larger harbours where there are undisturbed sandy and muddy areas. In these situations it may be as shallow as 10m.

V. mirabilis is most commonly found on northern and western coasts. Southerly records are very limited but populations are found in very sheltered locations, including Holyhead harbour, Portland Harbour and Plymouth Sound.

KEY FEATURES A slim unbranched colony, in mud.

SIMILAR TO Tall hydroids can look similar to sea pens but the mud habitat should distinguish this species from anything else. *Funiculina quadrangularis* (p. 46) is a much larger colony.

Loch Etive, Argyll & Bute.

Garvellachs,
Firth of Lorn.

Pennatula phosphorea Phosphorescent Sea Pen

Left: 'Front' side of a colony. Sound of Shuna, Argyll.

Opposite: 'Rear' side view of a very red colony showing sclerites. Eigg, Small Isles, Highland.

The most stout and fleshy of the three British and Irish sea pens. The branches are triangular in cross-section and arranged alternately on opposite sides of the central stalk, rather than in pairs. As its name suggests it is capable of blue/green luminescence when stimulated. Its main stalk is white but the branches and polyps are pale pink. This species has sclerites in the body that are deep red giving the colony not only its strength but also its reddish overall colour. It is a particularly beautiful animal, all the more so for being found in often dark and muddy conditions.

Pennatula phosphorea is able to retract into the sediment in which it lives. It is also sometimes found bent over in a partly limp state when not actively feeding.
KEY FEATURES A broad, branched colony in mud.
SIMILAR TO There is nothing similar in British and Irish waters.

TG

Stoloniferans
Octocorallia, Order Stolonifera

The stoloniferans, like the soft corals, are octocorals and their polyps have eight fringed tentacles. The individual polyps arise from a slender, more or less tubular stolon. The British and Irish species are very small and easily overlooked, hence distribution information is patchy.

The taxonomy of stoloniferans is not straightforward. There appear to be two genera in British and Irish waters, *Sarcodictyon* and *Cervera* which are distinguished by the presence of sclerites in *Sarcodictyon* and their absence in *Cervera*. However this is not a distinction which can be made underwater.

Sarcodictyon catenatum and *Sarcodictyon roseum*

These two species both form an encrusting network of 2mm wide flattened stolons on rocks and shells, from which the polyps arise singly. The difference between the two species is based on microscopic features which would not be visible underwater, although the polyp length of *Sarcodictyon catenatum* (4–6mm) is greater than *Sarcodictyon roseum* (2–3mm). At present it is unclear if both species occur in British and Irish waters, however Richard Manuel's samples from the UK are of *Sarcodictyon catenatum*. In the absence of preserved material it is safest to record sightings as *Sarcodictyon* sp.

Each polyp is up to 6mm tall, including its tentacles and is semi-translucent white in colour. The stolon is typically red but it may be white or colourless. It is often overgrown with other life and only the polyps are visible.

Sarcodictyon spp. grow on rocks, stones and shells. They are occasionally found in shaded places on the lower shore but are more commonly encountered below low water mark and have been recorded as deep as 100m. They are found on all coasts of Britain and Ireland but are easily overlooked because of their small size.

KEY FEATURES Tiny translucent groups of polyps arising from an encrusting stolon.

SIMILAR TO *Alcyonium hibernicum* (p. 32) has similar sized polyps but they are arranged more densely together rather than along a stolon. Can also be confused with the sessile stage of jellyfish (p. 22).

A line of polyps rising from a red stolon.

Cervera atlantica / Cornularia cornucopiae

There are records from the shore in Portland, Dorset of a species with polyps are up to 20mm tall and a stolon which is much more slender than that of *Sarcodictyon catenatum/roseum*. This species was identified by Manuel (1981) as *Conularia cornucopiae*, which is a relatively well known Mediterranean species. Later work on the same specimens by López-González *et al.* place them as *Cervera* cf. *atlantica*.

Other Stoloniferans

Another stoloniferan has been recorded on a number of occasions from St Kilda, Scotland, but not elsewhere. This forms clusters of polyps which are denser than those of *Sarcodictyon catenatum/roseum*. The polyps rise from longish extensions to the stolon which are often covered in small particles, giving a rough surface. This is unlike *S. catenatum/roseum* where the polyps rise almost directly from the stolon.

Two pictures of the undescribed stoloniferan from St Kilda, (left) with polyps extended and (below) with polyps contracted, showing the stolon.

Tube anemones
Hexacorallia, Order Ceriantharia

Tube anemones are the only group of anemones to live in a felt or parchment-like tube buried in sand and mud. They all have two series of tentacles – short labial tentacles around the mouth and a larger number of longer marginal ones on the edge of the disk. The anemone can move within the tube, which has a smooth and slippery lining, enabling it to retract rapidly when disturbed. Unlike most anemones they cannot retract the tentacles into the soft column. Retracting the whole animal into the tube has the same effect. The tube is commonly much longer than the animal itself. The juveniles are planktonic and free swimming. Once settled the tube is constructed from many discharged nematocyst threads and mucus-bound external material.

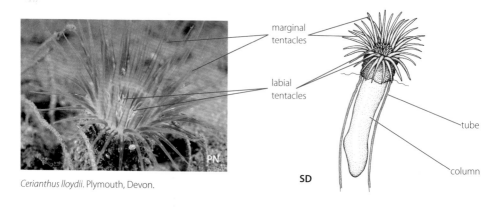

marginal tentacles

labial tentacles

tube

column

Cerianthus lloydii. Plymouth, Devon.

PN

SD

The two sets of tentacles are often different colours though rarely as strikingly contrasted as this Fireworks Anemone *Pachycerianthus multiplicatus*. Loch Hourn, Highland.

TG

Cerianthus lloydii Burrowing Anemone

Much the most common and widespread of the tube anemones. It has up to 70 marginal tentacles which may have a span of 70mm. The colour of the tentacles is very variable and mixed colours often occur in same area.

Cerianthus lloydii has a widespread distribution. It is usually found in soft sediments – sand and mud, but can also occur in gravel, maerl and rarely amongst pebbles and cobbles. It occasionally occurs on the lower shore but is usually sublittoral, being found to depths of 100m or more.

KEY FEATURES Two sets of tentacles, living In a parchment tube, which may be buried In sediment.

SIMILAR TO Smaller and with fewer tentacles than *Pachycerianthus multiplicatus* (p. 54) and much more common.

Two differently coloured specimens from Plymouth (top) and South Uist (above).

Pachycerianthus multiplicatus Fireworks Anemone

Two *Pachycerianthus multiplicatus* showing the variability in colour and banding of the tentacles. Loch Hourn, Highland.

This is one of the largest sea anemones in British and Irish waters and is a spectacular sight, particularly since it contrasts with the muddy seabed in which it lives. It has up to 200 marginal tentacles with a span of up to 300mm and lives in a tube which may be up to 1m long. The marginal tentacles are whitish, sometimes with brown bands, and are characteristically held with the base part upright and the ends flowing in whatever water movement there may be, giving them a very graceful appearance.

Pachycerianthus multiplicatus has a very restricted distribution in Scotland and Ireland, and is only found in soft mud in very sheltered situations towards the head of sea lochs and similar inlets.

P. multiplicatus is vulnerable to the impacts of scampi and scallop dredging and is a Priority Species in Scotland.

KEY FEATURES A large graceful anemone only found in soft mud in Scottish sea lochs, and more rarely in similarly sheltered sites in Ireland

SIMILAR TO Larger and with more tentacles than *Cerianthus lloydii* (p. 53).

Above: The column and tube of this specimen are clearly visible. Loch Duich, Highland.

Right: A partly closed anemone showing how the long tentacles curl when retracting. Loch Duich, Highland.

Fireworks Anemone *Pachycerianthus multiplicatus* Surveys 2005–2013

Seasearch divers have carried out surveys of *Pachycerianthus multiplicatus* populations in several Scottish sea lochs since 2005. *Pachycerianthus multiplicatus* was targeted because of its restricted range in British and Irish waters and the susceptibility of populations to physical damage from fishing gear, both towed and static. Since the anemones live in muddy sediments and mostly below 15m depth, the level of knowledge of the extent and numbers in the population was very low and Seasearch aimed to improve on this through the use of trained volunteer divers.

In many ways *Pachycerianthus multiplicatus* are an ideal project for SCUBA survey. They are found in sheltered locations, they are large and easy to identify, and experienced divers with excellent buoyancy control can work close to fragile creatures and an unstable seabed more easily than other survey methods.

Surveys have been carried out in the following sea lochs:

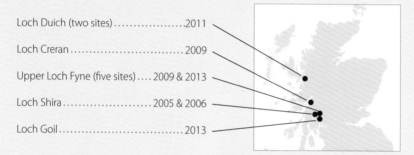

Loch Duich (two sites) 2011

Loch Creran 2009

Upper Loch Fyne (five sites) . . . . 2009 & 2013

Loch Shira . . . . 2005 & 2006

Loch Goil 2013

The methodology used to record the populations was for pairs of divers to swim out from the shore on a compass bearing until they reached a maximum depth of 30m or until their dive time reached 20 minutes. They would then turn at right angles to the shore, swim approximately 10m parallel to the shore then turn again to head back to shore recording as they went. In this way each pair of divers recorded two transects running from the shore to their maximum depth.

During each transect the number, depth and size of each *Pachycerianthus multiplicatus* was recorded.

Pachycerianthus multiplicatus do not generally cluster together. These two specimens are fluorescing producing dramatic colours. This may be a response to the light of the diver's torch or camera strobe.

Light coloured *Pachycerianthus multiplicatus*. Loch Shira, Argyll.

Large populations were recorded in Loch Shira, at three of the sites in Upper Loch Fyne, one site in Loch Duich and at Loch Goil. All of these share a number of characteristics:

- A muddy seabed.
- A significant source of fresh water input which periodically deposits large amounts of organic matter in the form of leaves, twigs, soil etc.
- Signs of periodic low oxygen episodes, either *Beggiatoa* mats or black anoxic layers near the surface of the sediment.
- Limited or no competition from other burrowing fauna such as sea pens, *Nephrops*, *Mya* sp.
- Some protection from mobile gear and no or limited static gear fishing.

This is an on-going survey project and in future years Seasearch hopes to:

- Revisit the Loch Fyne and Loch Shira sites surveyed in 2009 to see if changes in the size distribution observed at one site between 2009 and 2011 is replicated elsewhere.
- Carry out more surveys in Loch Goil to discover if the site reported here is typical of the Loch Goil population as a whole and if there is any variation in the size distribution of the anemones.
- Place markers beside several anemones and revisit at regular intervals to obtain information about growth rate and longevity.
- Explore other sites with similar characteristics to see if *Pachycerianthus multiplicatus* populations are more widespread than currently known.

References

Pachycerianthus Survey – Loch Shira October 2006.
Paisley, O. 2007 – available online at www.seasearch.org.uk

Fireworks Anemone distribution in West Scotland 2009–2013.
Paisley, O. 2013 – available online at www.seasearch.org.uk

Pachycerianthus indet. 'Dorothy'

Sark, Channel Islands.

This anemone is very similar to *Pachycerianthus multiplicatus* (p. 54), though it is not quite so large. It has up to 150 marginal tentacles with a span of up to 200mm. The tentacles are much less likely to be banded but there is a dark brown area at the base which seems to be a consistent feature. Unlike *P. multiplicatus* it is found in areas of rock and gravel rather than mud.

The taxonomic status of this anemone is uncertain and it does not appear to have been formally described or named. The name Dorothy is an affectionate name coined by Richard Manuel for an individual specimen in an aquarium. There is a similar species in the Mediterranean known as *Cerianthus membranaceus*.

There is no overlap in distribution between the two British species and the only part of Britain and Ireland from which this species is known is the Channel Islands. It also occurs on the adjacent coast of Brittany.

Arachnanthus sarsi

Above: Firth of Lorn, Argyll and Bute. Below: Rathlin Island, Antrim.

Arachnanthus sarsi has the fewest tentacles of the British tube anemones, 30 inner labial ones and 30 long marginal ones. The inner labial tentacles are held together pointing upwards to form a cone which is characteristic of the species. The whole animal may protrude up to 200mm from the tube. It is found in sand or shelly mud at depths from 10–36m. It may be partly nocturnal, a feature of other anemones of this genus found in tropical waters.

This is a very rare anemone which has been only recorded from a few sites in western Scotland and north and north-west Ireland. Because of its rarity and its vulnerability to trawling and dredging it is a Priority Species in Scotland and Northern Ireland.

KEY FEATURES Graceful tube anemone found in mud and muddy sand.

SIMILAR TO Fewer tentacles than any other of the tube anemones.

Colonial anemones
Hexacorallia, Order Zoantharia

These colonial anemones consist of a number of polyps growing from an encrusting conenchyme attached to rocks and stones. This part of the colony is often covered over with sand or bryozoan or hydroid 'turf'. The polyps of the different species are very similar. The disc is a little wider than the column which gives a delicately fluted appearance to the polyp when looked at in profile. There are two circles of tentacles which are found on the edge of the disc, one of which is usually held up and the other flat.

The colonies grow in size by budding off new polyps from the common base. This is known as extratentacular budding. New colonies are formed from the distribution and settlement of planula larva.

inner ring of tentacles

outer ring

fluted column

concave disk

basa coenenchyme

closed polyp

SD

There are four species of British and Irish zoantharians in this book which are regularly recorded, two of which *Epizoanthus couchii* (p. 61) and *Isozoanthus sulcatus* (p. 65) are quite small and easily overlooked. There are also a number of other species that have only been found in very deep waters offshore or for which there are no recent records.

Epizoanthus couchii Sandy Creeplet

A cleaner and more colourful colony. Isle of Man.

Close up showing the long tentacles and detritus around the base. Plymouth, Devon.

The polyps of this colonial anemone are small, up to 10mm tall and 5mm in diameter, and arise from a thin narrow base which is attached to rock or shells and is often covered in sand or other detritus. The tentacles are translucent white with a tiny white tip and the remainder of the body semi-translucent buff or pinkish. There are between 24 and 32 tentacles and the column has a serrated parapet.

Epizoanthus couchii is found on rocks and shells and sometimes forms extensive networks which seem to attract sandy particles, hence its English name. Although widespread on southern and western coasts it is easily overlooked because of its small size, subdued colour and tendency to retract the polyps.

KEY FEATURES Groups of small polyps with long semi-translucent tentacles. Colonial, but the common base is usually covered with particles of detritus.

SIMILAR TO This species is smaller and less obvious than the two species of *Parazoanthus* (pp. 62–64) and has proportionally longer tentacles. It could also be confused with small soft corals or stoloniferans but these have only eight fringed tentacles on each polyp.

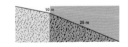

Epizoanthus papillosus and *Epizoanthus incrustatus*

There are two known forms of these anemones. One grows over gastropod shells and completely replaces the shell over time. There are up to 20 polyps in each colony each of which is up to 15mm tall and 6mm in diameter. The other form has little or no basal encrustation and the polyps either radiate from a central point or bud from the walls of others. The polyps are thought to be similar to *Epizoanthus couchii*. Both anemones are inhabitants of sand and gravel and found in depths of 20–200m. Both have been recorded in the past from a number of different localities around British coasts and further afield from both sides of the North Atlantic. *E. papillosus* is found in dredge samples and is associated with hermit crabs but neither species is likely to be recorded by divers.

Parazoanthus axinellae Yellow Cluster Anemone

Parazoanthus axinellae, a typically yellow cluster. Penzance, Cornwall.

This colonial anemone forms dense clusters of polyps arising from a common base which is normally visible. Its colour is usually pale yellow with a contrasting area of much darker yellow or orange around the mouth. However it can be white. There are up to 34 slender and pointed tentacles on each polyp and the polyps are up to 15mm tall.

    Parazoanthus axinellae is found both on rocky and organic surfaces in depths from 6–100m. It is most commonly encountered by divers on rocky surfaces in 20–30m. It prefers shaded surfaces just out of strong currents and may be near the base of the rocks close to sand but just above the scour zone.

    P. axinellae is a generally southerly species in Britain and Ireland and also occurs around south-western Europe and in the Mediterranean. Because of its rarity in the north it is a Priority Species in Scotland and Northern Ireland.

KEY FEATURES Dense clumps of yellow polyps, but occasionally white.

SIMILAR TO Pale colonies can be confused with *Epizoanthus couchii* (p. 61). However the tentacles are shorter in relation to the body and *P. axinellae* does not retract so readily when disturbed, making it an attractive photographic subject.

    White colonies can be confused with *Parazoanthus anguicomus* (p. 64) however the latter has shorter tentacles and has a more spreading colony form.

Parazoanthus axinellae may also have a pinkish hue and often grows on other living surfaces, as here with the Crumpled Duster Sponge, *Axinella damicornis*. Isles of Scilly.

Here yellow and white colonies of *Parazoanthus axinellae* are growing side by side. Plymouth, Devon.

Parazoanthus anguicomus White Cluster Anemone

Part of an extensive area of *Parazoanthus anguicomus*. Sound of Mull.

Parazoanthus anguicomus is the largest of the colonial anemones with polyps up to 25mm tall and up to 44 tentacles which are not much longer than the width of the disk. The polyps are not very densely arranged and the colonies often form extensive sheets rather than discrete clumps. Colonies are usually found in dark locations such as overhangs, crevices, the roofs of caves or on wrecks. The colour is dull to bright white.

    P. anguicomus is largely a northern species and it is possible that many of the southern records are misidentifications and are actually white *Parazoanthus axinellae*.

KEY FEATURES White, extensive colonies often in shaded places.

SIMILAR TO *P. anguicomus* is similar to white coloured *P. axinellae* (p. 62) but can be distinguished by its less densely clustered growth form, larger polyp size and more robust appearance with proportionally shorter tentacles.

Isozoanthus sulcatus Ginger Tiny

Stoke Point, Devon.

A distinctive little anemone, also known as Peppercorn Anemone. Dark brown in colour and commonly found in areas where there is a thin layer of silt over rock. Its polyps are only 4mm tall and 2mm in diameter and have between 19 and 22 tentacles. The common base of the colony is usually covered in fine silt or other debris. The polyps often stand out against their silty surroundings but they are very shy and will retract if disturbed.

Isozoanthus sulcatus is found in open rockpools on the lower shore and in the shallow sublittoral on silted rock, stones and shells.

KEY FEATURES Groups of tiny brown polyps in thin sediment over rock.
SIMILAR TO No similar species. Once seen it is unmistakable.

Anemone predators

The stinging nematocysts possessed by all of the anemones can be used to ward off would-be predators as well as to entrap potential prey. However they are not effective against all comers.

Most of the nudibranchs, or sea slugs, are specialised predators and a number of different species prey on anemones, in addition to those that prey on hydroids.

There are five *Tritonia* spp. nudibranchs in our waters all of which prey on anothozoans. Two of them, *Tritonia hombergi* and *Tritonia plebeia*, feed on *Alcyonium digitatum* (p. 28).

T. hombergi is a large and distinctive nudibranch with a range of arborescent processes and tubercules along the back and sides of the animal. Juveniles can be seen dotted about on the soft coral fingers whilst the larger ones hide in nearly crevices when not actually feeding. *T. plebeia* is a much rarer species.

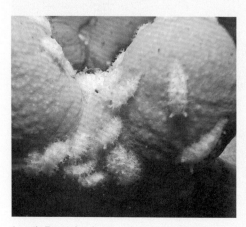

Juvenile *Tritonia hombergi* on *Alcyonium digitatum*.

Tritonia plebeia grazing on *Alcyonium digitatum*.

Tritonia nilsodhneri spends most of its life on Pink Sea Fans, *Eunicella verrucosa* (p. 36), though it can sometimes be seen on the seabed presumably looking for a new sea fan host. The animal itself is well camouflaged, especially when the sea fan has its polyps extended, but the coils of eggs laid around a sea fan branch are distinctive. Unlike the anemone also found on sea fans, Sea Fan Anemone, *Amphianthus dohrnii* (p. 129), the presence of the nudibranch seems not to do any lasting damage, and new polyps are presumably budded off to replace those eaten.

The abundance of *T. nilsodhneri* on sea fans varies from year to year. At The Manacles in Cornwall Seasearch surveys showed a big drop in numbers from being present on 47% of fans counted in 2004 to only 4% in 2006. Recent counts in 2012 found them on 21% of 250 sea fans counted.

Tritonia nilsodhneri adult and egg mass on *Eunicella verrucosa*.

Aeolida papillosa feeding on *Anemonia viridis*.

The Aeolid nudibranchs feed on hydroids and anemones and many of them are able to pass undischarged nematocysts from their prey through their digestive tract and onto the tips of the numerous cerata to be used in defence.

Aeolidia papillosa, the largest of the group, eats a wide variety of anemones, including *Anemonia viridis* (p. 92) as in the image above. *Aeolidiella glauca* tends to be found in sheltered muddy sites where it feeds on *Sagartiogeton* spp. both *S. undatus* and *S. laceratus*. *Aeolidiella sanguinea* feeds on *Sagartia*-type anemones, especially *Sagartia elegans* (p. 81), whilst *Aeolidiella alderi* also feeds on *Cereus pedunculatus* (p. 117) and *Diadumene cincta*. (p. 103)

Armina lovenii is a distinctive nudibranch with lines along its body. It is found in muddy habitats and is thought to feed on *Virgularia mirabilis* (p. 47).

It is not only nudibranchs amongst the molluscs that feed on anthozoans. There are two closely related little false cowries that live on sea fans and Dead Men's Fingers, *Alcyonium digitatum* (p. 28). *Simnia patula* is the species found on *A. digitatum* and often the little dark disc-shaped egg masses are more easily seen than the false cowrie itself. *Simnia hiscocki* has only recently been described as a separate species. It has a slimmer shell and lives on *Eunicella verrucosa*.

References

Seasearch Pink Sea Fan Surveys 2004–2006.
Chris Wood. Marine Conservation Society – available online at www.seasearch.org.uk

A Field Guide to Nudibranchs of the British Isles
Bernard Picton and Christine Morrow. Out of Print.

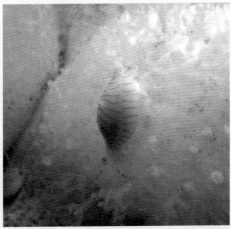

Simnia patula on *Alcyonium digitatum*.

Sea anemones
Hexacorallia, Order Actiniaria

This is the largest of the groups of anemones and corals, the sea anemones. The taxonomic order of the species does group similar species together by physical features, but in some cases there are other environmental clues which are more helpful to somebody looking at the species in their natural habitat. They have therefore been broadly arranged in four different groups. These are:

Sea anemones that usually occur in **groups or aggregations**, and related spp.

Sea anemones that live on the **shore or in shallow water**

Sea anemones that live on **soft seabeds**

Sea anemones that live on **other animals**

This division is a guide and some species do not fit in to it well. These species are placed with similar species with which they might be confused.

PN

An example of a sea anemone which usually occurs in groups, *Metridium dianthus* the Plumose Anemone, seen here in the Isles of Scilly.

Sea anemones that usually occur in groups or aggregations, and related species

Most of this group of anemones usually occur in closely spaced groups. They are not colonial animals but individual anemones which cluster together, usually as a result of their reproductive strategy. Also included here are some closely related anemones which have physical similarities but are not found in groups.

Protanthea simplex Sea Loch Anemone

Part of a cluster of *Protanthea simplex* in Loch Linnhe, Argyll & Bute.

A northerly species which is common in Scottish sea lochs but nowhere else in Britain and Ireland. It is also known from much deeper water, up to 400m, around Rockall and in Scandinavia.

Protanthea simplex is a delicate and attractive looking species with long slender tentacles which, unusually, cannot be retracted into the column. There are up to 200 tentacles with a spread of up to 70mm. They are translucent white with a somewhat frosted appearance. The column is smooth and flared at the top with a translucent white or light pink colour.

The anemone has an unusual 'collapse' behaviour in which it loses all muscular strength and hangs limply down from the attached disk. This is a temporary behaviour and presumably represents a resting phase that in other anemones would be accompanied by retracting the tentacles into the column. It is also often only loosely attached and can become detached from the rock and move through the water with jerky movements of its tentacles

It is a sociable anemone and in suitable locations there may be many individuals close together. In a Scandinavian survey a density of 2000 anemones per square metre was observed. It is found on open rock faces and other firm surfaces such as wrecks, sea squirts and worm tubes.

KEY FEATURES A bright white anemone only found on hard surfaces in sea lochs.

SIMILAR TO A very distinctive anemone. *Gonactinia prolifera* (below) is much smaller.

Left: Floating *Protanthea simplex* in mid-water. Loch Goil, Argyll & Bute.

Below: A 'collapsed' specimen alongside normally erect anemones. Loch Linnhe, Argyll & Bute.

Gonactinia prolifera

A tiny anemone, only 5mm tall, including the tentacles, and has about 16 non-retracting tentacles which are relatively large. The colour is a translucent white or pink. It is well known for its swimming ability though is normally found attached to seaweeds, worm tubes or sea squirts. It is a rarely recorded anemone with British records from Plymouth, Northern Ireland and Scottish sea lochs and islands.

KEY FEATURES Small size, non-retracting tentacles.

SIMILAR TO Smaller than *Protanthea simplex* (p. 69) and with fewer tentacles.

An anemone in the process of reproducing by transverse fission. A second column and set of tentacles has been produced prior to breaking away from the original anemone below. Loch Carron, Highland.

Urticina felina Dahlia Anemone

A typical group of differently coloured *Urticina felina* on rock with a layer of coarse sand. The closed specimen to the left has sand sticking to the column. St Abbs, Borders.

The two species in the family *Urticina* are two of the larger of the British sea anemones. *Urticina felina* is the more common and is up to 20cm across the tentacles, which are short and stout and arranged in multiples of ten. The column is covered in small grey warts, which usually have gravel or shell fragments attached to them as on the closed anemone above. The colour is very variable and the disc may be either plain or patterned with the tentacles banded or plain and often contrasting in colour from the disk. Different colour forms may occur together. *U. felina* generally reproduces sexually, though lateral fission has been observed. Hence there is not the same clustering of individuals of the same colour as with species which habitually reproduce by laceration or fission.

U. felina is found both on the lower shore and sublittorally down to at least 100m. It occurs on rocks, shells and stable gravel seabeds and may form dense carpets in crevices, gullies and wave-exposed locations. In such situations it can represent a high proportion of the biomass. It is an active feeder on anything that comes within range of the stinging nematocysts. This can include prawns, young fish or even something as large as a jellyfish.

It is a slow-growing and long-lived species. Although there is little information from *in situ* observations, aquarium specimens have been known to live for over 50 years.

U. felina is a very widely distributed anemone and may occur in cool temperate areas all around the northern hemisphere. In the US it is known as the Northern Anemone. It is common around all of the coasts of Britain and Ireland.

KEY FEATURES A large, wide anemone with numerous short plump tentacles banded in a variety of colours. Adhesive warts on the column.

SIMILAR TO *Urticina eques* (p. 73) which grows to a larger size and does not have adhesive warts. *Stomphia coccinea* (p. 75) has adhesive warts but the base of the column is wider than the span of the tentacles

Different colour patterns of *Urticina felina*. Left from Sheephaven, Donegal and right from Selsey, Sussex.

TG

Urticina felina ingesting a sea mat covered kelp blade. South Harris, Hebrides.

Urticina eques Horseman Anemone

This anemone is placed here in this guide because it is very similar in shape and variety of coloration to *Urticina felina* (p. 71) and the two species are easily confused. *Urticina eques* grows larger, up to 35cm across the tentacles. Its tentacles are similarly stout, though they may be a little longer, and are also arranged in multiples of ten. The main difference is in the column which in the case of *U. eques* does not have adhesive warts and consequently does not have gravel and other fragments attached to it. There are small pale spots on the column but these are not adhesive. Though there is a good deal of variety of colour the column, disk and tentacles often have shades of pink or red on them. A streaked form with patches of red and buff on the column, as in the picture below, is common.

U. eques is exclusively sublittoral, but occurs in the same sorts of habitat as *U. felina*, often in gullies and at the base of rocks where they meet sand and gravelly areas. The two species can often be seen together.

U. eques is less widespread than *U. felina*.

KEY FEATURES A large anemone with short, usually banded, tentacles and a smooth column without sand and gravel attached.

SIMILAR TO The two *Urticina* species can be confused, especially where the they occur together, but the size, colour and lack of warts on the column are usually sufficient features to confirm the identity of *U. eques*.

A pink and buff specimen with a typically red-streaked column. Loch Nevis, Highland.

A closed specimen with a red column, smooth and without any gravel attached. Holderness Coast, Yorkshire.

Two pictures of the same white *Urticina eques*, expanded and closed. St Abbs, Borders.

Stomphia coccinea Swimming Anemone

Left: The broad column and the upward held tentacles are both visible in this picture from Loch Etive, Highland.
Right: A closed specimen showing the broad base and a covering of silt. St Abbs, Borders.

Stomphia coccinea is included here because of its close similarity to the two preceding species though it does not occur in groups. Its English name comes from the ability of anemones of this group, in response to approaches by starfish, nudibranchs or other predators, to release their hold on the substratum and perform jerky movements with the extended column allowing them to move clear of danger. Other members of the family which occur elsewhere in the world, are better able to do this than this particular species which has only been observed to jump clear of the seabed momentarily.

S. *coccinea* has a broad base, often wider than the disk and which attracts particles of sediment. The tentacles are relatively short and characteristically arranged. There are six tentacles in the first ring and these are often held upwards over the mouth (compare with *Mesacmea mitchellii* p. 122). The colour is very similar to *Urticina eques*, with reddish hues and often with two red bands on the tentacles.

S. *coccinea* can be found on stones and shells, often on the large Horse Mussel, *Modiolus modiolus*. It is entirely sublittoral, occurring as deep as 400m. It has a wide distribution, occurring throughout the circumpolar regions of the northern hemisphere. Rarely recorded in our waters.

KEY FEATURES Broad base to the column, wider than the spread of the tentacles. Short, banded tentacles with the inner ring held upwards.

SIMILAR TO *Urticina felina* (p. 71) and *U. eques* (p. 73). *S. coccinea* is smaller and with a very broad base to the column.

Bolocera tuediae Deeplet Sea Anemone

St Abbs, Borders.

Bolocera tuediae is a large anemone which is rather similar in size and form to the two large *Urticina* species, which is why it is included here. However it has a different colour and is found in different situations. It has up to 200 long tentacles which are usually held in a regular and graceful fashion. They have a slight constriction around the base of each tentacle and the anemone is capable of shedding tentacles by pinching them off by muscular action. The reason for this is not known. *B. tuediae* can grow to a large size, up to 30cm across the tentacles. The colour is usually white but it can be pink, buff or even orange. The tentacles are never banded and are the same colour as the column, which is also plain.

    B. tuediae is always found sublittorally, usually deeper than 10m. It has a northerly distribution in the British Isles, Gosse named it deeplet because the specimens he had were from deep water, though the diminutive -let is hardly appropriate for this large anemone.

KEY FEATURES Large white or pale pink anemone, northerly distribution.

SIMILAR TO *Urticina felina* (p. 71), *U. eques* (p. 73) and *Stomphia coccinea* (p. 75) but has longer, more graceful tentacles and is plain coloured without any banding.

Aiptasia couchii Trumpet Anemone

Lyme Bay, Dorset.

The Trumpet Anemone (originally Trumplet) is named after the shape of its long smooth column, which has a trumpet-shaped flute at the top. The tentacles, of which there are about 100, are long, stout at the base but taper to a fine point. Those closest to the mouth are longer than those on the edge of the disc. They do not usually retract though they are capable of doing so. The span of the tentacles is up to 15cm. The colour is a greeny-brown, often streaked with white or blue from the mouth across the disc to the base of the tentacles.

Aiptasia couchii is often found in large numbers where it occurs. It is one of the few anemones that is known to reproduce both asexually by transverse fission and also by viviparity.

It is found on the lower shore and sublittorally down to 100m. Divers see it most often in shallow water where it is attached to rocks, in crevices amongst boulders and cobbles or even attached to kelp holdfasts.

A. couchii is a southerly species in the Britain and Ireland. In recent years it has been known as *Aiptasia mutabilis* but this species is now thought to be confined to the Mediterranean.

It is nationally scarce, though where it does occur there may be large numbers.

KEY FEATURES Clusters of individual anemones in shallow water, streaks on the disk and long inner ring of tentacles. Southerly.

SIMILAR TO A distinctive anemone, unlikely to be confused with anything else.

Metridium dianthus Plumose Anemone

Two brightly coloured Plumose Anemones *Metridium dianthus* ('plumose' form) showing the smooth column with a parapet at the top and the mass of fine tentacles. Sound of Mull, Argyll & Bute.

Previously known as *Metridium senile*. *Metridium dianthus* in its most common form is a large and conspicuous anemone which is unlikely to be mistaken for anything else. However there is also a smaller form which is less distinctive. Both forms have an adhesive base which is wider than the column. The column is long and smooth and there is a distinct collar or parapet near the top. The tentacles are numerous and slender.

'plumose' form

The large 'plumose' form is the tallest sea anemone in British and Irish waters and may be up to 30cm in height, with a spread across the tentacles of 15cm. In older specimens the disc may be waved or folded forming lobes. The tentacles are short and there may be several thousand of them giving a characteristic fluffy appearance to the anemone. They are normally all one colour with little differentiation between the column and the disc, typical colours being white, orange and, less commonly, green. However, some individuals have an orange column with white tentacles.

'pallidus' form

The small 'pallidus' form does not exceed 25mm across. The disc is flatter, not waved as in the larger variety, and there are not normally more than 200 tentacles. The column is shorter, not usually any taller than it is wide. It is likely that the two forms are variants resulting from different environmental conditions.

M. dianthus is a very social animal and in favourable conditions there are often large numbers of individuals closely packed together. They often completely cover the sides of wrecks or harbour walls, if the water current is strong, and give them a completely white appearance. They are capable of movement by contraction and expansion of the base allowing them to slide along. This allows the colonisation of new areas. As an example if a mooring rope is tied to a wreck which has *M. dianthus* on it, they will soon begin to move up the rope to take advantage of the passing food in the current. One of the things that helps them to become dominant species in suitable habitats is their ability to use 'catch tentacles' to sting adjacent fauna and discourage colonisation (see p. 15).

Both sea spiders and the large nudibranch *Aeolidia papillosa* have been reported to predate on this species.

M. dianthus normally reproduce by basal laceration, though sexual reproduction also occurs. In basal laceration small pieces of flesh from the base of an adult anemone tear off and generate new animals around the base. It is common to see large individuals with a number of small ones around the base (see photograph below). Because of this method of reproduction there are often large numbers of one colour form together.

The large size of this anemone is partly because of its ability to pump itself up with water when feeding. When the current is slack the anemones often deflate and the tentacles are retracted inside the column, which is left with a small hole inside the contracted collar.

This is a very common anemone and occurs from the lower shore to 200m depth. Elsewhere in the world it occurs on both the Pacific and Atlantic coasts of North America. It has been introduced to the Adriatic Sea and South Africa. The small '*pallidus*' form is more common on the shore and in shallow waters, including brackish creeks and estuaries. The large 'plumose' form is exclusively sublittoral.

KEY FEATURES 'Plumose' form: long smooth column with parapet and many short fine tentacles.

SIMILAR TO The 'plumose' form is a distinctive anemone, unlikely to be confused with anything else. The dwarf '*pallidus*' form could be confused with a number of other small anemones but the smooth column with a parapet is distinctive if visible.

A group of white coloured *Metridium dianthus* ('plumose' form), some expanded and some contracted. There are many tiny anemones clustered around the base of the columns of some of the larger specimens. Hand Deeps off Plymouth.

An aggregation of small *Metridium dianthus* (*pallidus* form) in two colours. Farne Islands, Northumberland.

Sagartia elegans Elegant Anemone

Sagartia elegans showing three varieties, *venusta*, *rosea* and *nivea*. Eddystone, Devon.

A common anemone but one which is very variable in colour and consequently easily confused. The tentacles are relatively long and up to 200 in number, rather irregularly arranged and consequently not as 'neat' in appearance as many anemones. The column, visible in closed specimens, has numerous pale suckers, which appear as whitish spots. These spots are not adhesive and, unlike many anemones with suckers on the column, they do not have particles of sand or shell attached to them. The span of tentacles is up to 40mm.

There are five recognised colour varieties, which were originally thought to be separate species, and a number of other colour forms.

Variety *miniata* is the most widespread form. The overall colour is between brown, buff and orange with the disk and tentacles with similar colours and often variegated. The tentacles are usually banded and a common variation has a rayed appearance with light lines from the mouth across the disk and onto the tentacles.

Variety *rosea* has bright pink or rose red tentacles, often with a lighter disk. It is a bright and prominent anemone and unlikely to be confused with anything else.

Variety *nivea* has both the disk and tentacles bright translucent white in colour.

Variety *venusta* has a bright plain orange coloured disk with contrasting white tentacles.

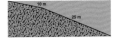

Variety *aurantiaca* is the rarest colour variety and may be a south-westerly

variety – records are from south Wales and Devon. The disk is greyish in colour with dull orange tentacles

Sagartia elegans are found attached to rocks on the shore and down to 50m depth. Shore specimens are found in pools, under stones, in caves or beneath overhangs. They commonly occur in crevices or holes into which they can withdraw if disturbed.

Sublittorally they are found on open rock surfaces often in very large numbers packed closely together. They reproduce primarily by basal laceration and thus the large groups are normally all of one colour variety. A typical habitat in south-western England is at the top of vertical rock faces where the topmost metre of the cliff is covered with *S. elegans* and the remainder equally densely covered with *Corynactis viridis*.

S. elegans is both common and widely distributed around all coasts of Britain and Ireland. In Europe it is found north to Scandinavia and Iceland and south into the Mediterranean.

KEY FEATURES Attached to rocks and stones, often in large numbers. Column has light coloured, non-adhesive warts.

SIMILAR TO The different colour forms can be confused with a number of other species. Usually the non-adhesive warts on the column are the best feature to distinguish them.

Variety *miniata* is most easily confused with *Sagartia troglodytes* (p. 114) and *Cereus peduncluatus*

Above: The white non-adhesive warts on the column are diagnostic. St Kilda.

Right: Variety *miniata*. Farne Islands, Northumberland.

(p. 117) but both of these are normally found in sand and gravelly areas rather than rock. Both of these other species also have adhesive suckers on the column and normally have fragments of sand and shell attached.

Variety *nivea* could be confused with white specimens of *Actinothoe sphyrodeta* (p. 84) but has many more tentacles, is neater in appearance and has white suckers on the column whereas there are lines along the column of *A. sphyrodeta*.

Variety *venusta* could also be confused with the 'fried egg' form of *Actinothoe sphyrodeta* (p. 84), but again the column is quite different.

Variety *aurantiaca* is very similar in appearance to the '*decorata*' colour form of *S. troglodytes* though the habitat and presence of adhesive suckers in the latter should distinguish them.

KH

Above: Variety *rosea* with small numbers of variety *nivea* and *venusta*. Runnel Stone, Lands End.

Left: Variety *venusta*. Sutherland, Highland.

Actinothoe sphyrodeta White-striped Anemone

A cluster of open and closed 'fried egg' form of *Actinothoe sphyrodeta*. Isles of Scilly.

Also known as the Sandalled Anemone, but White-striped Anemone is thought to better describe the anemone's appearance. It has plain colours and up to 100 irregularly arranged tentacles which have a stout base and taper to the tips. The size is up to 50mm across the span of the tentacles. The column is smooth, without suckers or other features. It is rather uneven in colour, often with longitudinal patches of pure white on a duller background forming stripes. There are two colour forms to the disk and tentacles. Most commonly both are bright white but some have an orange disk with white tentacles (the fried egg form).

Actinothoe sphyrodeta reproduces asexually by longitudinal fission and often occurs in groups. These do not tend to be so closely packed as *S. elegans* (p. 81) nor do they cover large areas. This anemone is almost entirely sublittoral, though it may occasionally occur in overhanging situations on the lower shore. It is normally found on open rocky surfaces but may also attach to other firm surfaces such as kelp holdfasts. It likes water movement and can tolerate turbulent conditions.

KEY FEATURES Attached to rocks and stones, often in loose groups. Column smooth and usually striped, without warts.

SIMILAR TO Similar in appearance to two of the varieties of *Sagartia elegans* (p. 81). The white form could be confused with *S. elegans* var. *nivea* and the fried egg form with *S. elegans* var. *venusta*. The two distinguishing features are the column, which does not have suckers and often has longitudinal lines and the smaller number of tentacles with a tapering form and less tidy appearance.

Left: Open and closed anemones clearly showing the lines on the column. Coll, Hebrides.

Below: The white form of *Actinothoe sphyrodeta* showing the long and less tidy tentacles which help distinguish it from *Sagartia elegans*. Plymouth, Devon.

Settling on the *Scylla*

The sinking of an ex-Navy frigate HMS *Scylla*, in Whitsand Bay west of Plymouth, in March 2004, provided an opportunity to record the colonisation of species on a new metal wreck structure. Seasearch was involved in the recording and a paper was produced which incorporated all of the records made during the first five years after the sinking and from which the following information is taken.

SSh

Sagartia troglodytes was an early coloniser, seen here in the first summer. Numbers subsequently reduced.

One of the earliest anemone colonizers was Mud Sagartia *Sagartia troglodytes* (p. 114), occurring frequently by mid-summer 2004 and still present at the end of 2008. Plumose Anemones, *Metridium dianthus* (p. 78), characteristic of wrecks in the area, were first observed in late summer of the first year.

Elegant Anemones, *Sagartia elegans* (p. 81), also a characteristic species of steel wrecks in the area, were first seen in mid-summer 2005 and by the end of the summer in 2006 were well established with large groups and all of the different colour varieties present. The Dahlia Anemone, *Urticina felina* (p. 71), which was abundant on *Scylla* on arrival from Portsmouth, was first seen at the end of August 2006. It is not a common species off Plymouth and numbers remained low on the wreck for the rest of the study period although, based on observation of visible individuals, there may have been some increase in abundance after summer 2008.

Jewel Anemones, *Corynactis viridis* (p. 135), were first observed in summer 2004 when they had already started to form patches of many individuals produced by asexual division and therefore of the same colour. They occurred mainly on the outer part of the vessel but also inside.

The Devonshire Cup Coral, *Caryophyllia smithii* (p. 138), was first observed in September 2005. The coral was still only occasional on the wreck after five years and only one has been seen colonised by the barnacle *Megatrema anglicum*, which lives only on stony corals.

The common Dead Men's Fingers soft coral, *Alcyonium digitatum* (p. 28), was first observed in early summer 2005 and grew to nearly full size in one year although it had only just started to branch in summer

2006. By early 2009, *A. digitatum* had become a visually dominant part of the reef community. The more unusual Red Sea Fingers soft coral, *Alcyonium glomeratum* (p. 30), which occurs on other wrecks in the area as well as on rocky reefs, was first observed in April 2007. It remained occasional on the wreck at the end of the study.

Pink Sea Fans, *Eunicella verrucosa* (p. 36), which are a major feature of the marine life on most wrecks in the area, were especially searched for and eventually found on 12 August 2007, in the fourth year after the sinking. There also appeared to be a settlement in summer 2008. *E. verrucosa* occur on the bedrock reefs within 50m of *Scylla*. Growth was initially rapid and by the end of the first winter, individuals were up to 6cm high and some had started to branch. By winter 2008–2009 the largest individuals were about 17cm high and some had several branches.

By the end of five years the anthozoan community was largely typical of other metal shipwrecks in the area with a predominance of Dead Men's Fingers and Plumose Anemones. However, there were species missing which have colonised other local wrecks, such as Pink Soft Coral, *Alcyonium hibernicum* (p. 32), and hard corals were poorly represented with only *Caryophyllia smithii* present in small numbers, whilst *Caryophyllia inornata* (p. 140) and *Hoplangia durotrix* (p. 141) remained absent.

A young *Eunicella verrucosa* in August 2008.

References

Colonisation of an artificial reef in south-west England – ex-HMS *Scylla*.

Keith Hiscock, Sally Sharrock, James Highfield and Deborah Snelling. 2010. *Journal of the Marine Biological Association of the United Kingdom* 90(1), 69–94.

The upper superstructure of the *Scylla* dominated by *Alcyonium digitatum* and *Metridium dianthus* with patches of *Corynactis viridis* and *Sagartia elegans*.

Sea anemones that live on the shore or in shallow water

The following anemones all normally occur on the lower shore, in rockpools and in shallow water. Other species that occur below low water can also sometimes be found in the shallows and on the shore.

Actinia equina Beadlet Anemone

Two *Actinia equina* of different colours, side by side. Sark, Channel Islands.

Actinia equina is one of the most common anemones of the shore and intertidal pools. It is frequently seen as a red jelly-like blob left on rocks that the tide has exposed or as expanded anemones in rockpools. Its colour is usually a deep red but it may also be various shades of brown, orange or green. The anemone is normally a single colour with no differentiation between the column and tentacles. However some specimens may have blue or yellowish spots or streaks on the column. It often has a hump in the centre of the disk which elevates the mouth.

The name beadlet is taken from the ring of, usually bright blue, acrorhagi around the rim of the column. These are hollow warts which are filled with nematocysts and thus can have an aggressive function.

A. equina does not reproduce asexually, unlike many anemones. Instead it reproduces viviparously, producing fully formed young individuals which are born through the anemone's mouth.

Whilst this anemone can be found in the shallow sublittoral it is normally encountered between the high and low water mark. It can be attached to any firm structure, normally rock, but may also be on wooden or metal piles or concrete breakwaters. It can tolerate reduced salinity and thus also occurs in brackish situations.

A. *equina* is very widespread throughout Western Europe from Russia in the north to West Africa.

The different colour forms of beadlet anemones were for many years thought to be a single species. However two other closely related species, *A. fragacea* and *A. prasina*, are now recognised and it is possible there may be others.

KEY FEATURES Shore and shallow water species, single colour, usually red and with a smooth column in the same colour.

SIMILAR TO The three species of *Actinia* in our waters all live in similar habitats. Red specimens with an evenly coloured column will be *A. equina*. Green specimens are similar to *A. prasina* (p. 91) but have more tentacles.

Actinia equina exposed at low tide. Whitsand Bay, Cornwall.

A red specimen showing the ring of acrorhagi or nematocyst filled warts which give it its common name. Sark, Channel Islands.

Actinia fragacea Strawberry Anemone

Open and closed specimens on the lower shore. Wadham Beach, Devon.

Actinia fragacea is similar in form to *A. equina* (p. 88) but grows to a larger size, 80mm across the base and 100mm across the tentacles. It is always red or dark red in colour and has small flecks or spots of green, yellow or blue over the whole of the column, giving it its English name. The tentacles are plain red. Unlike *A. equina* it is not known to reproduce viviparously.

A. fragacea is found in on the lower shore and often in shaded places. Like *A. equina* it may be attached to any suitable firm structure.

This anemone is much less common than the *A. equina* and has a more restricted distribution.

KEY FEATURES Shore and shallow water species, with a distinctive strawberry-like column.

SIMILAR TO The colour pattern of the column is distinctive.

Actinia prasina

Actinia prasina has only been identified as a separate species as recently as 1984. It is light green in colour and has 100–160 irregularly arranged tentacles, rather than 192 in *A. equina* (p. 88). The specific name comes from the latin *prasinus* meaning leek-green. It occurs on the shore but, like *A. fragacea* (p. 90), usually lower down than *A. equina*. It also prefers dark, overhanging, surfaces and is rarely found on open rock.

    A. prasina was identified from specimens in the Isle of Man and it has also been found in Morecambe Bay. It is not known if it occurs elsewhere. Anemones in the family *Actinia* show significant genetic differences from different locations as a result of their viviparous reproduction. There may therefore be a number of genetically differentiated species, especially from island locations.

KEY FEATURES Shore and shallow water species, green coloration.

SIMILAR TO Easily confused with green specimens of *A. equina*. This species has fewer tentacles and may be restricted to the Isle of Man and adjacent waters.

Both photos Isle of Man.

Anemonia viridis Snakelocks Anemone

A large, colourful *Anemonia viridis*. Selsey, Sussex.

One of the most common and distinctive anemones of the lower shore and shallow sublittoral. The tentacles are long, irregularly arranged and up to 200 in number. The size is very variable but may be up to 18cm across the tentacles. The tentacles are sometimes plain coloured, from a grey-brown to fairly bright green and many specimens have bright purple tips due to the presence of symbiotic algae. Occasionally the anemone is seen with longitudinal purple stripes along the tentacles.

Like its relative on the shore *Actinia equina* (p. 88), the tentacles readily latch on to any invasive object, and the stickiness can be felt with a fingertip. The column is very variable in height, often totally obscured by the tentacles, which cannot retract, but when it can be seen it is reddish or dark brown, occasionally with lighter longitudinal streaks.

Anemonia viridis commonly reproduces by longitudinal fission and consequently there are often a number of individuals close together. It is found in rockpools on the lower shore and attached to rocks, stones or occasionally seaweeds down to about 20m. It enjoys exposed places and is often seen in areas of strong wave action or strong current. However it can also be found in sheltered areas such as seagrass beds.

There is considerable variation in size and appearance of anemones in different habitats. Those specimens growing on seagrass stems are uniformly smaller, grey in colour and with smaller numbers of tentacles, whereas those on

rock and other hard substrata may grow to a larger size and show the full range of colour variation.

The Snakelocks Anemone was formerly known as *Anemonia sulcata*. This is also currently identified as a valid species but there is considerable confusion between records of the two and whether they are either a single species or both part of a species complex containing a number of different species. It is possible that the small anemones found on seagrass are a different species to the larger ones on rocky substrata. *A. viridis* can provide a refuge for small spider crabs and prawns (pp. 94–95).

KEY FEATURES Many long untidy tentacles which do not retract.

SIMILAR TO The larger and more brightly coloured specimens are distinctive. Small specimens can be confused with a number of similarly sized anemones, such as the *Sagartia* spp., but usually have a plain grey colour without specks, flecks or bands, which is distinctive.

A small grey Individual on seagrass. Dingle, Co. Kerry.

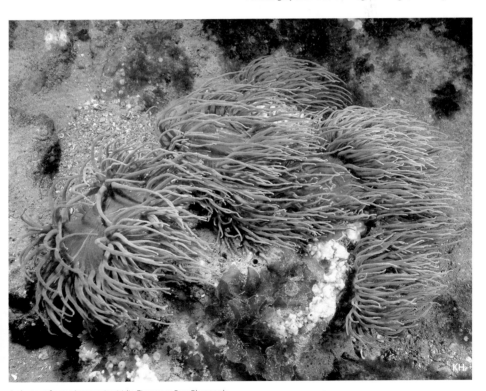

A cluster of grey *Anemonia viridis*. Firestone Bay, Plymouth.

Living with Snakelocks

There are symbiotic relationships between Snakelocks Anemones, *Anemonia viridis* (p. 92), and two species of crustaceans in our waters, Leach's Spider Crab, *Inachus phalangium*, and the Snakelocks Shrimp, *Periclimenes sagittifer*.

Inachus phalangium is one of three closely related species of *Inachus* or sponge spider crabs found in our waters. They are difficult to tell apart *in situ* but *I. phalangium* is probably the only one that associates with *A. viridis*.

The crab is commonly found around the base of the anemone, though it may be seen sitting amongst the tentacles. Not all Snakelocks Anemones have spider crabs associated with them but for those that do the anemone provides shelter from predators and the crab may perform a cleaning function for the anemone. There is normally not more than one crab per anemone and they leave the anemone at night to feed and also to moult.

Observations in the Mediterranean have shown that *I. phalangium* can walk between the tentacles of *Anemonia sulcata* and *Aiptasia mutabilis* without prompting a feeding response by the anemone.

SD

Inachus phalangium is commonly found in association with *Anemonia viridis*, but often hides under the disk rather than, as here, amongst the tentacles. Jersey, Channel Islands.

Periclimenes sagittifer Snakelocks Shrimp, is one of over 150 species of *Periclimenes* throughout the world. Most are found in tropical waters and they associate with a number of different species, including anemones, sea urchins, nudibranchs and starfish. In each case the shrimp benefits from the protection of the host species but whether they offer anything in return is unclear. Tropical anemone shrimps are known to venture out of the anemone to clean parasites off fish but it is not clear if they perform a cleaning function for the anemone. There is an aquarium study which recorded shrimps eating the tips of the tentacles of the host anemone.

P. sagittifer is thought to be the only representative of the family in the North-east Atlantic. Until 2007 its range was thought to extend from Northern France and the Channel Islands as far south as Gibraltar. However in that year it was recorded by Seasearch divers Matt Doggett and Polly Whyte from Swanage Pier, the first record from the British mainland. A Seasearch survey in October 2008 found shrimps in 7.5% of the anemones at Swanage, and as in 2007 they seemed to be present only in the autumn.

There were no Seasearch records from the British mainland in 2009 but in 2010 they were seen between June and October at four sites from Swanage westwards towards Weymouth. Also the first, and only, sighting from Sussex was made at Selsey. In 2011 the first sightings were in April and came from Portland, where

The first record of *Periclimenes sagittifer* in Devon, Babbacombe.

P. sagittifer was found on both sides of the island. In October 2011 the first mainland record from west of Dorset came from Babbacombe in Devon, almost 50 miles away on the other side of Lyme Bay. There have been no further records from Devon but in 2012 *P. sagittifer* was seen at two sites in Dorset, in May and July.

For the time being *P. sagittifer* remains a rarely recorded species on the north side of the English Channel but it appears to have spread both eastwards and westwards since the first record in 2007 and also become present over a longer period during the year. It remains much more common in the Channel Islands where in 2010 a Seasearch survey at a site in Sark found that 13% of Snakelocks Anemones contained a shrimp, roughly twice the density of the survey in Swanage.

It is interesting that both of these species associate with *A. viridis* rather than other species, though associations have also been reported with *Aiptasia mutablis* in the Mediterranean, and *Inachus* spp. spider crabs are found in a variety of habitats. *A. viridis* is one of the larger shallow water anemones and importantly is one which does not retract its tentacles. It thus offers full time protection which other species would not be able to do. *A. mutablis* also rarely retracts its tentacles. All records of this species should be reported.

References

Snakelocks Anemone Shrimps, *Periclimenes sagittifer*, Swanage Pier, Dorset, 2008
Polly Whyte and Matt Doggett – available online at www.seasearch.org.uk

Distribution of the Anemone Shrimp *Periclimenes sagittifer* in Maseline Harbour, Sark
David Kipling – available online at www.seasearch.org.uk

Periclimemes sagittifer at the base of *Anemonia viridis*. Sark, Channel Islands.

Anthopleura ballii Red Speckled Anemone

RS

A brightly coloured specimen showing the flattened disk and flecks on the tentacles. Isles of Scilly.

Anthopleura ballii varies in overall colour from yellow to brown and is usually flecked with specks of grey and white, especially on the tentacles. There is a fairly broad flat disk and up to 96, relatively long, tentacles arranged in multiples of six. They are somewhat untidily arranged and often curled over at their tips.

The column Is distinctive. It can be long and trumpet-shaped when fully extended and has longitudinal rows of small, non-adhesive warts. These are pale and each is tipped with a dark red spot. The overall colour of the column is similar to that of the disk.

Sublittorally the anemone is often found buried in sand and mud and attached to a firm object beneath the surface. It is a common inhabitant of seagrass beds. On the lower shore and in pools it occurs in holes or crevices amongst rocks, particularly in old piddock borings or beneath boulders.

This is a southern species which is also found in France, south-west Europe and the Mediterranean.

KEY FEATURES Flattened disk with white flecked tentacles. Long column with red-tipped non-adhesive warts.

SIMILAR TO *Aulactinia verrucosa* (p. 98), but generally larger and the dark red spots on the column of this species are diagnostic, though small and best seen in a close up image. *Anthopleura thallia* (p. 99) is a similar size and occupies the same habitats but has adhesive warts on the column.

A paler specimen of *Anthopleura ballii*. Mulroy Bay, Donegal.

Column of *Anthopleura ballii* showing non-adhesive dark red-tipped warts. Dingle, Kerry.

Aulactinia verrucosa Gem Anemone

Expanded anemone in a typical habitat with a thin layer of sand over rock. Alderney, Channel Islands.

Aulactinia (formerly *Bunodactis*) *verrucosa* has rather bright tentacles which are white but spotted or banded with grey. There are up to 48 tentacles arranged in multiples of six with a span of 60mm. The disk is patterned and variously coloured including green, red and brown. The column is distinctive since it has longitudinal lines of warts. It is pink or grey and most of the warts are darker. However the six main rows are white. The warts in this species are non-adhesive and it never has pieces of sand or shell attached.

    A. verrucosa reproduces sexually and produces fully-formed young. It is found mostly on the shore in pools or in clefts amongst rocks, or attached to rock or stones covered with sand. It is primarily a south-westerly species in Britain and Ireland though there are occasional records from the north and east.

KEY FEATURES A small shore and shallow water species, with distinctive white rows of non-adhesive warts on the column.

SIMILAR TO Other rockpool species have warts, such as *Anthopleura thallia* (p. 99), but the white lines on the column are distinctive.

Closed anemone showing the distinctive lines of warts on the column. Jersey, Channel Islands.

Anthopleura thallia Glaucus Pimplet

A typical rockpool group of anemones showing the gravel attached to the column. Whitsand Bay, Cornwall.

Anthopleura thallia has vertical rows or warts on the column, those at the top of the column, the parapet, being larger than those lower down. They may join together to from a knobbly ridge. Unlike *Anthopleura ballii*, the warts on this species normally have fragments of shell and gravel attached. The tentacles, of which there are up to 100, are rather stiffly held and irregularly arranged. The disk usually has a pale plain circle around the mouth and then a dark pattern on a variegated background. The tentacles can be olive green or grey and speckled with white or plain white and grey. The column is a dull green, brown or grey, sometimes reddish and the warts may be either lighter or darker than the colour of the column itself. There is usually a darker longitudinal line joining the rows. The anemone has a span of 50mm across the tentacles and the column can also be extended to 50mm.

A. thallia is almost always found on exposed rocky shores, from mid-tide level to low water. It will be found in pools, crevices or amongst mussel beds. If there is any gravel present it may well bury itself completely in it. This can make it a difficult anemone to find.

KEY FEATURES Rockpool species, flecked tentacles and prominent adhesive warts. Often partly buried in sediment

SIMILAR TO Other similar shallow water species such as *A. ballii* (p. 96) and *Aulactinia verrucosa* (p. 98), have non-adhesive warts.

A 'clean' specimen showing the column and adhesive warts. Aquarium image of specimen from North Devon.

Cataphellia brodricii

Isles of Scilly.

This anemone is one of the Hormathid anemones, most species of which are found living on other animals. This one, however is usually encountered on the lower shore and shallow sub-littoral. Here it may be attached to stones, beneath boulders, around kelp holdfasts, or on rocks with a thin sand covering and often in areas with a moderate current. It is very sensitive to disturbance and retracts quickly making it difficult to find.

Cataphellia brodricii has a wide base, up to 60mm across, which often exceeds the span of the tentacles and a column covered with small solid tubercules. The disc and tentacles have a delicate pattern in yellow, cream and brown. The tentacles are relatively short, arranged in five cycles and up to 96 in number.

C. brodricii is a southerly species which is rarely recorded.

KEY FEATURES Small anemone in shallow water with column covered In tubercules.

SIMILAR TO Phellia gausapata (p. 106) is similar both in habitat and appearance but there is little or no overlap in distribution and P. gausapata has a pinkish coloration. Other anemones in similar habitats can also have a mottled coloration, such as Anthopleura thallia (p. 99), Anthopleura ballii (p. 96) and Aulactinia verrucosa (p. 98) and it is necessary to look at the column and the pattern of the disk and tentacles to make a confident identification.

Sagartia ornata

Sagartia ornata amongst mussels. Egersund, Norway.

This anemone until 1987 was considered to be a variety of *Sagartia troglodytes* (p. 114) and thus information on its distribution is rather limited.

It is a small anemone found on the lower shore and in shallow water, often amongst mussels. The overall colour is green or brown and the tentacles are characterised by pale bands. There is a series of pale spots around the mouth and at the base of the tentacles. Like all of the *Sagartia* anemones it has warts on the column.

KEY FEATURES A small *Sagartia* anemone with pale bands on the tentacles and white spots around the mouth

SIMILAR TO Smaller than *Sagartia troglodytes* and usually in a different habitat.

Aiptaisiogeton pellucidus

Pink specimens in an aquarium.

A very small anemone. It has a smooth column and relatively long slender tentacles, which do not generally retract. It reproduces by basal laceration and as a consequence the base often has a rather ragged outline. It also means there may be a number of individuals of different sizes close together. There appear to be two colour forms, one translucent orange with whitish patches at the base of the tentacles and the other with deep pink tentacles.

Aiptaisiogeton pellucidus lives attached to rocks in holes and crevices from the lower shore down to about 10m depth. It appears to be rare and there are no recent records of it. However, it may well be under-recorded because of its small size. It is known from a few localities in Dorset and Devon and also further south to Biscay and into the Mediterranean. *Aiptasiogeton hyalinus*, which may be the same species, has been recorded from Oban.

KEY FEATURES A tiny anemone with smooth column and translucent orange or pink tentacles.

SIMILAR TO Easily confused with small anemones of other species, including *Diadumene cincta* (p. 103) and *Metridium dianthus* (p. 78).

Diadumene lineata Orange-striped Green Anemone

Diadumene lineata. Porthallow, Cornwall.

A small, delicate species with long tentacles. The column is distinctly divided into scapus and capitulum with the lower scapus coloured with orange, yellow or white stripes over a green or brown background. This contrasts with the upper part of the column, the capitulum, which is a translucent grey-green. The anemone is up to 40mm high, though it is often smaller. The tentacles are long and numerous, up to 100 in number. They are translucent, either colourless or pale grey-green usually irregularly flecked with white or grey. They contrast with the disk, which is darker.

Diadumene lineata is usually found in sheltered locations on the shore in pools attached to rocks and shells, frequently amongst mussels. It is tolerant of variations in temperature and salinity and frequently occurs in brackish creeks, lagoons, harbours and marinas. In the British Isles it has been recorded from a variety of sites including Chichester Harbour, the Tamar and Fal, Strangford Lough and as far north as Orkney.

D. lineata appears to have originated in the western Pacific and has since spread to many other regions. It is thought that its spread is likely to have been the result of being carried on ship's bottoms or transplanted oysters or other shellfish. Many of the locations are close to shipping lanes and present or former shellfish cultivation areas. Since the anemone normally reproduces asexually, by longitudinal fission, only a single specimen is required to start a new population.

This species has previously been named both *Haliplanella lineata* and *Diadumene luciae*.

KEY FEATURES Tiny anemone green column with orange lines.
SIMILAR TO No other species has a similarly coloured column.

Diadumene cincta Orange Anemone

capitulum

scapus

Above: A group of *Diadumene cincta* on chalk rock. Dover.
Left. Close up showing the column divided into scapus and capitulum.

A small delicate anemone with a slender column and translucent orange colour. Though it may be up to 60mm tall the disk is small, little wider than the column. The tentacles, of which there may be up to 200, are long and fine. The slender column is divided into two parts, a scapus and a capitulum, and when not fully extended may appear lop-sided due to irregular contraction. The colour is usually translucent orange but may have a greenish tinge, especially on the disk.

Diadumene cincta frequently reproduces by basal laceration and thus there may be large number of individuals close together. It also means that distribution can be very patchy. Where it occurs it is attached to some hard surface, particularly mussels and other bivalve shells. It occurs on the shore in pools and caves, but not in places which dry out at low water. It is a typical inhabitant of areas with reduced or variable salinity such as estuaries, tidal creeks and harbours. However, it can also be found as deep as 40m and is a common feature on shipwrecks in south-east and eastern England.

KEY FEATURES Small translucent orangey coloured anemone often found in large numbers together.

SIMILAR TO Can be confused with small specimens of *Metridium dianthus* (p. 78) which often occurs in the same habitats and may have an orange coloration. *D. cincta* however, is more elongate with the column divided into scapus and capitulum. It also has many fewer tentacles.

Diadumene cincta is often found on wrecks and seems to tolerate both strong currents and some sedimentation. It can look very like young Plumose Anemones, *Metridium dianthus*, as here on the *James Eagan Layne*, Whitsand Bay, Cornwall.

Phellia gausapata Olive Green Wart Anemone

A group of *Phellia gausapata* amongst tunicate, sponge and bryozoan turf. St. Kilda.

This anemone was originally called the Warted Corklet by Gosse. It typically occurs in small groups in extremely exposed shallow rocky situations, often in surge gullies in the kelp zone and usually on vertical surfaces. Most British and Irish records are from exposed sites in the north-west of Scotland and Ireland such as Shetland, St Kilda, Rockall, Rathlin and Achill Islands. There is also a recent record from the Isles of Scilly.

Phellia gausapata has up to 120 tentacles which are irregularly arranged. The disc and tentacles are orange, red, brown, or grey usually variegated colours, and the tentacles are vaguely banded. It is one of the Sagartiid anemones and the column is covered with dark rounded tubercules and a tough horny covering which typically has algae, debris or other animals (including bryozoans and worms) attached to it.

KEY FEATURES Anemones in groups in vertical shallow exposed habitats.

SIMILAR TO Similar to *Anthopleura thallia* (p. 99) which also has adhesive warts on the column. However there is little overlap in distribution.

Phellia gausapata showing the column, dark warts and *Crisia* bryozoan turf around the base. Sula Sgeir.

Family Edwardsiidae Worm anemones

There are seven British members of this family of anemones all of which have a long worm-like column with a rounded base. Most are small and difficult to see, retract quickly and may be at least partly nocturnal. Because of this they are probably under-recorded and we have not produced distribution maps, which could be misleading.

Edwardsiella carnea

SS

Above: A group of *Edwardsiella carnea* on rock. Right: Close up of *E. carnea*. Both Loch Carron, Highland.

This is the most widespread and common of the group. It is up to 30mm long and 4mm in diameter. The tentacles are long and slender, up to 32 in number and pinkish in colour whilst the disk has white or yellow markings. The column is divided into a scapus and scapulus. The lower scapus is covered in a thick brown cuticle and the rounded base has adhesive spots which it uses to attach to rocks. The upper scapulus is translucent and similar in colour to the disk.

RS

Edwardsiella carnea lives in holes and crevices in rocks, often in large aggregations. It has a particular preference for old Piddock borings. It occurs from mid-tide level to the shallow water offshore, usually found in sheltered spots out of the light. It is easily overlooked since if disturbed it retracts its tentacles rapidly, as it does if out of water.

E. carnea has been recorded from all British and Irish coasts, though records are few in number.

KEY FEATURES This is the only one of the worm anemones which is found in rocky areas.

SIMILAR TO Superficially similar in habitat, size and grouping to the stoloniferan *Sarcodictyon catenatum/roseum* (p. 50) but the tentacles are quite different, unbranched in the case of *E. carnea* and fringed along their length in *S. catenatum/roseum*.

Edwardsia claparedii, Edwardsia delapiae, Edwardsia timida and *Scolanthus callimorphus*

These four burrowing anemones live in mud, sand or gravel and are not attached. When *in situ* only the disc and tentacles can be seen. They live in sheltered locations in shallow water and may occur in large groups. They were often found in beds of the Eelgrass *Zostera marina* but since the decline of this habitat are now more often seen in shallow muddy sand areas.

	Edwardsia claparedii	Edwardsia delapiae	Edwardsia timida	Scolanthus callimorphus
NUMBER OF TENTACLES	16	16	16–32	16
TENTACLE ARRANGEMENT	8+8	8+8	3 cycles	5+11
TENTACLE SPAN	50mm	45mm	40mm	100mm
TENTACLE COLOUR	Transparent with white spots	Long, transparent and unspotted – almost invisible	Translucent pale orange – may have white tips	Translucent – brownish towards tips, spotted or banded with white
DISC COLOUR	Mainly white but may have a buff pattern	Translucent – patterned with white and brown	Translucent pale orange with opaque white or pale cream pattern	Patterned cream, buff and dark purplish-brown
HABITAT	Mud and sand, *Zostera* beds but also offshore	Sand and gravel, *Zostera* beds	Sand and gravel	Sand and gravel, *Zostera* beds
DISTRIBUTION IN BRITISH AND IRISH WATERS	Widespread – mostly western coasts	One location only – Valentia Island, Co Kerry	Few current-swept locations without wave action e.g. Menai Strait, Strangford Lough and Scottish sea lochs	Southern England, Channel Islands, west Wales and western Ireland but rarely recorded

 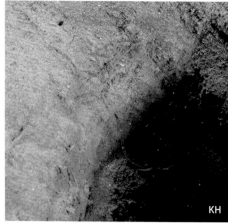

Left: *Edwardsia claparedii* with typically spotted tentacles and showing the characteristic 8+8 tentacle arrangement, Rathlin, Northern Ireland. Right: A translucent specimen demonstrating just how difficult this species is to find. Plymouth Sound.

Edwardsia timida with translucent tentacles (left). With dense white spots on face of tentacles (right). Both Menai Strait, Gwynedd.

Scolanthus callimorphus, showing both speckles and bands on tentacles (left). *Scolanthus callimorphus*, emerging from sediment and showing pattern on disk and column (right). Both Roskeeda, Galway.

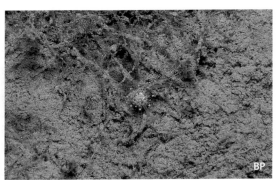

E. timida

Edwardsia delapiae. Valentia, Cork.

Starlet Sea Anemone *Nematostella vectensis* and Ivell's Anemone *Edwardsia ivelli*

Nematostella vectensis covering a muddy bottom and an individual anemone. Cley, Norfolk.

N. vectensis

These two anemones are both known only from brackish water lagoons in southern England where they occur burrowing in soft mud. Both are rare, and indeed *Edwardsia ivelli* is only known from one location in Sussex where it may now be extinct.

Both anemones are tiny, about 20mm long and 1.5mm in diameter with a span across the tentacles of 10mm, and where they occur may be in large numbers. *Nematostella vectensis* has been recorded at a density of over 10,000 per square metre. Both species occur in shallow lagoons and ponds, usually in depths of less than 1m. They live in fine sand and mud, often with shingle on top, and in the presence of green algae, especially *Chaetomorpha* spp. and Eelgrass *Zostera marina*.

Both anemones are highly vulnerable to disturbance whether by pollution, eutrophication, or physical damage by coastal defences or development. As a result they are both protected species under the Wildlife and Countryside Act.

KEY FEATURES Tiny anemones in muddy brackish water lagoons.

SIMILAR TO *Edwardsia* spp. but the brackish water lagoon habitat is unique.

Unidentified worm anemones

The availability of digital cameras and the number of keen underwater observers, many trained through and contributing to Seasearch, has led to a rapid increase in the exchange of photographs for identification purposes. Currently this is aided by the presence of Facebook Groups, including Seasearch Identifications (general) and NE Atlantic Cnidaria, where there is an active and rapid exchange of views on the less easy to identify species.

However, these groups cannot always come up with a definitive answer and some photographs remain unidentified. Two examples of images posted in 2013 are given below. Both are clearly in the family Edwardsiidae but, without specimens, that is a far as we can go based on the images alone.

This anemone has 18 tentacles in two cycles with alternate longer and shorter tentacles. It does not fit the description of any of the British and Irish species which either have 16 tentacles or the tentacles arranged in three cycles. It is also much more colourful than is normal for this group. It was photographed at Martins Haven, Pembrokeshire.

This anemone has the 16 tentacles typical of three of the species in this group. The tentacles are much less regular in length than the species above and it is brightly coloured. The orange coloration is reported for *Edwardsia timida* but this has 16–32 tentacles with four in the first cycle which is not apparent from this photograph. *E. timida* is typically found in current-swept situations and all of the records on the National Biodiversity Network are from northerly locations in Scotland and Northern Ireland with the most southerly record in the Menai Strait, North Wales. However the type locality is in northern France. This picture was taken at Brixham in south Devon.

Sea anemones that live on soft seabeds (sand, gravel and mud)

The following anemones all normally occur buried in sand, gravel and mud with only their oral disk and tentacles above the surface. There are two types; those that have their column attached at the base to a firm object in the sediment, whether a stone or shell, and the truly burrowing anemones which have a column that relies on its length and shape for stability and is not attached to anything in the sediment. Note that a number of the previous group of shore and shallow water species, especially the worm anemones, also live on soft seabeds.

Capnea sanguinea Imperial Anemone

Capnea sanguinea in a Horse Mussel, *Modiolus modiolus*, bed. Isle of Man.

Previously known as *Aureliania heterocera*. This is very distinctive anemone that is unlikely to be mistaken for any other because of its characteristic very short knobbed tentacles. There are up to 150 tentacles and the anemone is up to 70mm across. The colour is varied, often red, but it may be pink, purplish or yellow. Occasionally it is seen with white tentacles that contrast with the body colour.

Capnea sanguinea lives amongst cobbles and pebbles or with its column buried in sand, gravel or maerl. Its broad base acts as an anchor in the softer seabeds. It can retract its disk and tentacles very quickly and completely disappear from view.

This is an uncommon anemone and usually seen singly rather than in groups.

KEY FEATURES Short knobbed tentacles.

SIMILAR TO No similar species in our waters.

Multicoloured *Capnea sanguinea*. Top: Kilkieran Bay, Galway. Bottom: Loch Carron, Highland.

Sagartia troglodytes Mud Sagartia

A typically grey and white patterned specimen. Portland, Dorset.

A widespread and fairly common anemone which is very variable in colour and pattern, making identification more difficult than in many other species. It is normally found buried in mud, sand or gravel with its base attached to a buried stone or shell. However it may sometimes be seen on rocks, especially where they have a film of sand or silt over them. The specific name *troglodytes* is misleading as it suggests this is an anemone commonly found in caves whereas this would be a surprising habitat for it.

There are two similar anemones which were previously thought to be varieties of *Sagartia troglodytes* but are now recognised as separate species. What was previously referred to as the *decorata* variety is *S. troglodytes* and the other form is now *Sagartia ornata* (see p. 101).

S. troglodytes has up to 200 tentacles arranged in multiples of six. On some individuals the innermost ring of six tentacles is prominent and can be accentuated by a contrasting colour pattern. Where this can be seen it is a reliable identification feature, but it is not found on all specimens. The first ring of six tentacles usually has V-shaped markings at the base. Colour ranges from dull white through buff, brown and green and may have either plain or patterned disk and tentacles. As with all of the *Sagartia* anemones, the column has suckers and in this species often has fragments of gravel or shell attached to it.

This anemone is found on the lower shore and shallow waters and may occur in areas with reduced salinity such as harbours and estuaries.

KEY FEATURES A variably coloured *Sagartia* anemone found in gravel, sand and mud.

SIMILAR TO Other *Sagartia* anemones are usually found on rock (*Sagartia elegans*), or intertidally (*Sagartia ornata*). In its typical sediment habitat *S. troglodytes* is most likely to be confused with *Sagartiogeton undatus* (p. 118) but in this species both the column and tentacles are lined and the tentacles are longer. *Urticina felina* (p. 71), *Cereus pedunculatus* (p. 117) and *Mesacmaea mitchellii* (p. 122) are also found in similar habitats. The former two have a wide disk and short tentacles, whilst the latter has a characteristic way of holding the inner tentacles upwards and together at the tips.

An anemone with the inner tentacles held upright and successive rows becoming increasingly horizontal. Dingle, Co. Kerry.

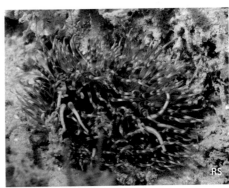

A purple colour form which seems more common in the south and east of England. Cley, Norfolk.

A colour form with a pattern of dark and light areas on the tentacles. Dingle, Co. Kerry.

An orange and brown anemone. Weybourne, Norfolk.

Sagartia troglodytes (left) next to *Urticina felina* (right) to aid comparison. Anglesey.

Anemonactis mazeli

Above: Specimen from north-west Spain.

Left: A juvenile from Strangford Lough, which lacks the knobbed end to the tentacles.

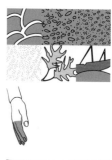

Anemonactis mazeli has 20 stout tentacles each of which has a constriction near the tip, which produces a rounded end. The tentacles are white or orange and usually have brown or purple flecks along them. The anemone is up to 6cm across the tentacles. The column is up to 12cm long and is normally buried in sand or mud.

This is a rare anemone with few records from the English Channel, The Irish Sea and Ireland, most recently from Strangford Lough and Loch Duich. It is usually found offshore from 20–650m depth.

KEY FEATURES Knobbed end to each tentacle, deepwater species.

SIMILAR TO No similar species in our waters.

Cereus pedunculatus Daisy Anemone

Cereus pedunculatus in shelly sand. Dingle, Co. Kerry.

Cereus pedunculatus is one of the larger sediment dwelling anemones and can be as much as 15cm across the disk. The tentacles are short and very numerous, up to 1,000 in a large specimen. The disk and tentacles are mottled in blue-grey and buff and often have minute white flecks. When partly contracted the disk tends to fold up at the edges. The column is trumpet-shaped with a wide base but this is not usually visible in life as the disk lays flat on the seabed and the column is buried.

This anemone occurs at all depths from pools and gullies on the lower shore to at least 50m. Where it occurs in muddy and sandy areas it will be attached to a buried object beneath the surface. In these situations there will often be many anemones in the same area.

KEY FEATURES Wide mottled disk and relatively short tentacles lying flat with column buried in sediment.

SIMILAR TO Similar to some specimens of *Sagartia troglodytes* (p. 114) both in colour and pattern but it is generally larger and the tentacles are shorter leaving a larger oral disk.

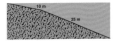

Sagartiogeton undatus

Sagatiogeton undatus without the column exposed. Brixham, Devon.

This anemone has a long column, up to 12cm in length, with a wide base. *Sagartiogeton undatus* is found buried in sand and mud, and the column is attached to a stone or shell beneath the surface. The column is often exposed, has a pale yellow coloration and stripes along its length. There are up to 200 long tentacles, which are arranged in groups of six and are held elegantly when fully expanded. They have a line along their length and are almost transparent towards the tips.

KEY FEATURES Tentacles with lines along their length. In sediment with yellow column, also lined.

SIMILAR TO Similar to *Sagartiogeton laceratus* (p. 120) but larger, with less colour and tidier tentacles.

Close up of tentacles showing the line along their length.

Sagartiogeton undatus with much of the column exposed. Dingle, Co. Kerry.

Sagartiogeton laceratus Fountain Anemone

Above: A closely packed group. Skye. Below: Anemones with young specimens around their bases. Loch Creran, Argyll.

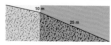

A relatively tall anemone with a column up to 60mm tall which flares out at the top to a disk which may be 30cm wide. The column and disk are orange or buff in colour and there is an intricate pattern of dark makings at the foot of each tentacle. There are up to 200 long tentacles. *Sagartiogeton laceratus* is often found in small groups, which is the result of its preferred method of reproduction by basal laceration.

This anemone may be found partly buried in sand and mud and attached to shells, worm tubes or rock beneath the sediment. It is exclusively sublittoral.

KEY FEATURES Trumpet-shaped column, untidy tentacles, orange disk

SIMILAR TO Similar to *Sagartiogeton undatus* (p. 118) but has an orange coloration, smaller in size and has less tidy looking tentacles.

Halcampoides purpureus Night Anemone

Left: *Halcampoides purpureus* in soft sediment. Jersey, Channel Islands. Above: In gravel.

A true burrowing anemone formerly known as *H. elongatus*. Its column has a rounded base, which is fixed firmly in the sand or gravel but is not attached to anything in the sediment. The column is at least 10cm long when not buried, but extends much longer when *in situ*. The oral disc is very small and the mouth is on a conical protrusion in the centre. There are 12 tentacles which are long and slim and capable of extension up to a span of 15cm. This is a distinctive anemone, which is widely distributed throughout the world, often recorded from great depths. It is probably much under recorded because it is primarily nocturnal and is retracted into the sediment during the hours of daylight. British records are from a number of widely distributed sites most of which are islands – the North of Mull, Kilkieran Bay, Galway, the Isle of Man, Skomer and the Channel Islands. It is exclusively sublittoral, being recorded from depths from 10m or deeper.

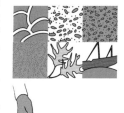

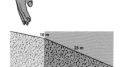

KEY FEATURES Twelve very long tentacles, only likely to be observed at night
SIMILAR TO *Peachia cylindrica* (p. 123) also has 12 tentacles and a similar coloration, however the *H. purpureus* tentacles are much longer.

Halcampoides abyssorum

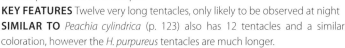

A very rarely recorded anemone which was originally described from deep water in the Norwegian and Barents Seas. Records from Britain and Ireland area are Skye, Northern Ireland, Lundy in Devon and Jersey, Channel Islands.
KEY FEATURES Long, translucent, trailing tentacles.
SIMILAR TO Mostly likely to be confused with a solitary hydroid rather than any other anemone.

Ardvasar, Isle of Skye.

Mesacmaea mitchellii Policeman Anemone

Lundy, Devon.

Mesacmaea mitchellii is a burrowing anemone which has a pear-shaped column with a rounded base. There are up to 36 tentacles, which are long and finely pointed at the tips. The first cycle of tentacles are seven in number and always held upwards and together, completely covering the mouth.

The anemone is up to 70mm across the tentacles and the disk and the tentacles are intricately patterned in shades of orange, brown and buff.

M. mitchellii is normally found burrowing in sand and gravel. It is rather a rare anemone, only being recorded from relatively few locations. However where it does occur there may be many individuals in the same area.

KEY FEATURES Inner tentacles held upwards and together at the tips.

SIMILAR TO Most other anemones found in sediment have many more or many fewer tentacles and the way the inner ring are held is a unique feature which makes *M. mitchellii* unmistakable.

Peachia cylindrica Clock Face Anemone

Above: Patterned specimen showing conchula next to mouth. Portrush, Northern Ireland.
Left: Specimen with white disk, a common coloration. Torquay, Devon.

PN

This is a burrowing anemone that lives with its column buried in sand and gravel but unattached. The column is elongated with a round base and may be as much as 30cm in length. The oral disc is small with a small lobed projection, called a conchula, arising from one side of the mouth. This is distinctive but difficult to see in live specimens underwater. There are 12 long tentacles with a span of up to 12cm. The tentacles are patterned in cream and grey with beautiful chevron markings. The disc may be the same colour or bright white.

Peachia cylindrica occurs from low water mark to at least 100m and is most common offshore. It is widely distributed around British and Irish coasts only being rare in the east.

KEY FEATURES Twelve tentacles, chevron marks on tentacles. Conchula on one side of the mouth.

SIMILAR TO Other anemones with 12 tentacles are *Halcampoides purpureus* (p. 121) and *Halcampa chrysanthellum* (p. 124). The former has very much longer tentacles and the latter very much shorter than this species.

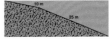

Halcampa chrysanthellum

A patterned specimen with two opposing cream tentacles. Valentia Island, Cork.

A small burrowing anemone with an elongated worm-like column up to 70mm long and buried in sand or mud. There are 12 short tentacles with a spread of about 10mm, which are patterned with alternate opaque and translucent lines. The disc is usually patterned in similar colours but may be yellow white or buff. There are often two opposite plain tentacles. In Strangford Lough the anemones are all white.

Halcampa chrysanthellum is most frequently found in or around Eelgrass, Zostera marina, beds and many records are from sheltered localities. However, there are also records from deeper water offshore.

KEY FEATURES Twelve short tentacles in sediment.

SIMILAR TO Other anemones with 12 tentacles are *Peachia cylindrica* (p. 123) and *Halcampoides purpureus* (p. 121) but both are bigger anemones and the tentacles are much longer than those of *H. chrysanthellum*.

A specimen with pale tentacles. Carmel Head, Anglesey.

Sea anemones that live on other animals

Most of the following anemones normally occur in association with other animals. The relationship differs but none of them use their host for food (i.e. they are not parasitic) and in two cases the relationship is a positive one for both partners (i.e. commensal). They are all in the family Hormathiidae and most have a tough leathery texture to the column, which has a wide base often used to adhere to organic substrates, whether alive or dead.

Calliactis parasitica Parasitic Anemone

This hermit crabs' shell is invisible beneath the anemone and barnacles. Start Point, Devon.

This rather inappropriately named anemone is usually found living on the shells of hermit crabs, in Britain the Common Hermit Crab *Pagurus bernhardus*. Often there may be more than one anemone on a single hermit crab shell. The relationship between the two species is a commensal, or sharing one. The anemone benefits from the mobility of the Hermit Crab and access to food. The crab benefits from the protection from predators afforded by the stinging nematocysts of the anemone. This species normally attaches itself to suitable shells without assistance from the crab but elsewhere other hermit crabs actively seek out anemones and place them on their shells. Sometimes the anemones can be found attached to other shells, including bivalves, and occasionally on other hard non-organic surfaces.

Calliactis parasitica has a long column and numerous fine tentacles which are not strongly coloured or patterned. They may be up to 700 in number. The column is a dull yellowish in colour with brown and reddish patches and spots, usually forming vertical stripes.

C. parasitica has a very restricted south-westerly distribution in British and Irish waters.

KEY FEATURES Tough leathery column, usually attached to hermit crab shells.

SIMILAR TO Unlikely to be mistaken for anything else when seen on hermit crabs.

Above: Here four anemones are attached to a single hermit crab's shell. St Mawes, Cornwall.

Calliactis parasitica attached to wreckage. The leathery column is distinctive. Plymouth, Devon.

Adamsia palliata Cloak Anemone

Hermit Crab *Pagurus prideaux* showing tentacles of *Adamisia palliata* under the body. Oban, Argyll and Bute.

Adamisia palliata lives in association with hermit crabs, in this case the Anemone Hermit Crab *Pagurus prideaux*. The anemone has a very wide base, which is modified to wrap around the hermit crab's shell. The disk and tentacles are underneath the shell and crab and the base covers the shell, meeting over the upper part. For identification therefore this is one anemone where it is the base and column which needs to be recognised as the disk and tentacles may be hidden underneath. The tentacles are very close to the mouth of the hermit crab, an ideal location for gathering scraps. The colour of the column is distinctive being white with chestnut shades and almost always covered with pink spots. The tentacles are relatively short and white in colour.

The relationship between the two species is apparently obligatory and neither is seen without the other. This is in contrast to *Calliactis parasitica* (p. 125) where, though it is almost always seen on a hermit crab shell, *Pagurus bernhardus* often occurs without the anemone. The presence of the anemone means

that *P. prideaux* does not have to change shells as it grows, a dangerous process. *A. palliata* produces a membrane which effectively increases the capacity of the shell as the crab grows. Its stinging tentacles also offer protection from predators. The anemone also readily emits nematocyst-bearing acontia as an additional protective mechanism.

A. palliata is widely distributed, but there is uncertainty over the correct scientific name. In the first edition of this guide, and a number of other sources it was called *Adamsia carcinopados*, however the World Registry of Marine Species currently considers this to be a dubious name.

KEY FEATURES Obligatory association with Anemone Hermit Crab, *Pagurus prideaux*. Column (on top of shell) with pink spots.

SIMILAR TO There are no similar species.

Above: Threatened crab with anemone emitting acontia. Firestone Bay, Devon.

Right: Purple spots on the column of *Adamsia palliata*. Oban, Argyll and Bute.

Amphianthus dohrnii Sea Fan Anemone

Multiple anemones on Pink Sea Fan *Eunicella verrucosa*. Whitsand Bay, Cornwall.

Amphianthus dohrnii lives almost exclusively on the two species of sea fans found in British and Irish waters, though it has been known to occur on other rod-like living structures such as hydroid stems. There is no benefit to the host animal from this association but presumably the anemone benefits from being elevated above the seabed into food-bearing currents. A Seasearch study has shown how it can damage Its host (see p. 131).

This is a small anemone which rarely exceeds 10mm across the disk. The base is modified to wrap around the stem of the host and the whole body may be elongated along the same axis as the stem it is attached to. The tentacles are relatively short and may be up to 80 in number. The colour is buff to pale orange and the tentacles are translucent white. This anemone normally reproduces by basal laceration which often results in a number of individuals being found on a single host.

Numbers of *A. dohrnii* appear to vary from year to year and it may have a much shorter lifecycle than its host. It also occurs in south-western Europe and in the Mediterranean and may be declining throughout its range. There are related species which have a similar lifestyle in tropical waters.

Because of the rarity of this species and its possible decline it is a Priority

Species in England and Scotland. Action taken to protect the Pink Sea Fan *Eunicella verrucosa* or Northern Sea Fan *Swiftia pallida* would also benefit the Sea Fan Anemone.

KEY FEATURES Normally found on sea fans, *Eunicella verrucosa* (p. 36) and *Swiftia pallida* (p. 42), usually with a number of individuals on one fan

SIMILAR TO Occasionally other anemones occur on sea fans, usually around the base. However this anemone is unlikely to be mistaken for any other in its usual habitat.

Multiple *Amphianthus dohrnii* on Northern Sea Fan *Swiftia pallida*. Firth of Lorn, Argyll & Bute.

Can Sea Fan Anemones damage sea fans?

The Sea Fan Anemone *Amphianthus dohrnii* (p. 129) is found almost exclusively on the two species of sea fans in our waters, Northern Sea Fan *Swiftia pallida* (p. 42) and Pink Sea Fan *Eunicella verrucosa* (p. 36). It is a priority species because of its rarity. In order to find out what effect, if any, the presence of these anemones have on their host sea fan Sally Sharrock of Devon Seasearch has carried out a six-year photographic monitoring survey of a single sea fan on the wreck of the Rosehill in Whitsand Bay, Cornwall.

Sally's research has shown that the anemones spread along the branch appearing to reproduce by basal laceration, smothering the sea fan polyps and the membrane that covers the skeleton thus killing the live tissue of the sea fan. Eventually they can weaken the fan structure enough that parts fall away. This could be accentuated by the weight of silt and turf attracted.

SSh   July 2006

Pictures of the same sea fan taken in July 2006 and May 2011. The second image shows a very weakened, lop-sided fan with a section on the left looking very vulnerable, attached to the main fan by a weak, dead looking connection. Interestingly the left hand section is feeding whilst the rest of the fan has retracted polyps. It is unusual for sections of a fan to be behaving so differently and it could be due to lack of connective tissue between the sections – thus the left hand section is behaving as an independent fan.

May 2011   SSh

By the end of the study the target sea fan had changed from a reasonably full and rounded shape to a lower oblong one, having lost most of the upper sections and with one section only barely attached. Lower sections where there were no anemones appeared to continue to flourish. However when the site was revisited in 2016 the entire colony had disappeared.

Perhaps in view of the damage they cause the host sea fan it is as well that *Amphianthus dohrnii* are rare. As both species are identified as priorities for conservation action, it would be ironic if one was a major cause of damage to the other. Because of the rarity of the *Amphianthus dohrnii* this is not the case.

References

Seasearch, Rosehill Sea Fan Anemone Project 2006–2012.
Sally Sharrock – available online at www.seasearch.org.uk

Hormathia coronata

Single specimen on rock. Loch Sunart, Argyll.

Hormathia coronata can be found living on shells or worm tubes but may also be attached to stones, rocks or objects buried in sand. It only occurs sublittorally where it may be found down to 100m. It has a broad base, which is up to 40mm across and may be up to 50mm high. The column has small solid tubercules. The tentacles are moderately long and arranged in multiples of six. The disk and tentacles are reddish or buff, usually with a delicate dark and light pattern. Reproduction is thought to be mainly by viviparity and consequently there are often small clusters of Individuals in the same area.

KEY FEATURES Sublittoral only. Column with solid tubercules.

SIMILAR TO *Stomphia coccinea* (p. 75) has a similar column but is normally larger and the tentacles shorter than *H. coronata*. The disk and tentacles of some colour varieties of *Sagartia elegans* (p. 81) are superficially similar but the column of *H. coronata* has solid tubercules rather than non-adhesive warts.

Two anemones, the right hand one closed up and visible only as a domed lump. Isles of Scilly.

Other rare hormathid anemones

There are four other rarely encountered hormathid anemones:

Hormathia digitata is a northerly species was previously frequent on the north-east coast of England but there are no recent records. It normally attaches to whelk and other gastropod shells, either alive or dead. A picture is shown from Norway to encourage recording in our area. For further information and pictures see Moen and Svensen 2004.

Hormathia digitata. Norway.

Hormathia alba is a deep water anemone which has been recorded off south-west Ireland.

Paraphellia expansa **Penny Anemone** lives buried in sand and shelly gravel and has a very wide base which is unattached and acts as an anchor. The column is often encrusted with sand, but does not have tubercules unlike *Hormathia coronata* (p. 132) and *Cataphellia brodricii* (p. 100). Records generally come from deepwater offshore locations on west coasts from Barra to south Devon.

Actinauge richardi is an unusual anemone in that it does not usually live attached to a hard surface, nor does it burrow deep into soft sediments. Instead its base is able to form an almost enclosed cup within which it encloses a ball of mud or sand. This allows it to live unattached with the ball acting as a sea anchor. It is a deep water anemone, always found offshore in depths of over 50m. It has a wide distribution but is not likely to be seen by divers.

Paraphellia expansa.

A patchwork of different colour groups of *Corynactis viridis*. Hatt Rock, Cornwall.

Corallimorpharians
Hexacorallia, Order Corallimorpharia

Corallimorpharians are effectively corals without a hard skeleton. Their internal anatomy, nematocysts and tentacles are identical to the hard corals. There are many tropical species but only one occurs in British and Irish waters.

Corynactis viridis Jewel Anemone

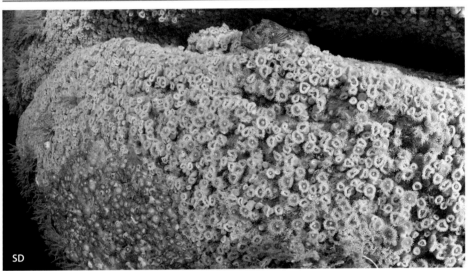

SD

Typically dense mass of *Corynactis viridis*. Sark, Channel Islands.

This is one of the most dramatic and often photographed of all the British and Irish anemones. Although each anemone is a separate individual they reproduce by longitudinal fission in which an individual first stretches itself and then splits across the middle creating two new anemones of equal size. This leads to large groups of densely packed cloned individuals on rock faces, often covering several square metres as shown in the image opposite. Individual anemones are up to 10mm across but have relatively long columns up to twice the width. When the tentacles are retracted they look like little coloured warts on the rock face.

Corynactis viridis are brightly coloured, ranging from pink (which looks blue underwater without a torch), through purple and bright emerald green to orange and brown, often with contrasting colours to the knobbed tips of the tentacles. These are colour varieties and not different species. Normally the colour varieties are found in groups rather than mixed, due to the reproductive process.

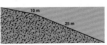

C. viridis have been recorded from the lower

shore and shallow waters where they are found in caves and under overhangs. However they are most common sublittorally, on vertical and overhanging rock faces as deep as 80m.

They are found in rocky areas along southern and western coasts and are particularly common on clear offshore reefs. Generally the anemones towards the southern extent of the range appear to be bigger than those in the north and they grow larger in conditions where there is a strong surge and clear water.

KEY FEATURES Easily distinguished from almost all other anemones by the knobbed end to each of its tentacles.

SIMILAR TO Cup corals also have knobbed tentacles but also have a hard skeleton.

Right: Side view of a single *Corynactis viridis* with contrasting tips to the tentacles and acontia present within the column. Sark, Channel Islands.

Below: Additional colour varieties from Harris, Donegal, Plymouth and Sussex. In the English Channel the most easterly records of *Corynactis viridis* are all on wrecks.

SD

KH

Hard corals
Hexacorallia, Order Scleractinia

As their name suggests these corals have a hard external skeleton and are also known as stony corals. Their tough exterior, known as a **corallum**, is secreted from the walls and base of the anemone-like polyp and is made almost completely of calcium carbonate. In times of danger, or when not feeding, the **polyp** can completely withdraw inside the hard outer cup and, also like an anemone, its tentacles contain stinging cells. The top and inside of the corallum comprises of a series of vertical radial plates or **septa** which correspond to the mesenteries of the polyp itself.

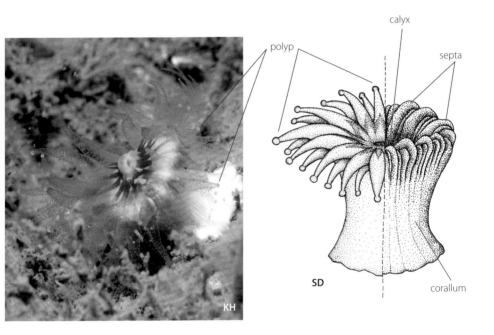

Some species of hard coral are solitary, living as separate individuals, although there may be many others of the same species nearby. Others consist of many corallites fused together to form a colony. All are slow growing and fragile. Hard corals reproduce by releasing eggs and sperm which combine in the water column to form free-swimming larvae. The colonial corals are also able to reproduce asexually by budding new polyps. Colonial corals are the reef-building corals of the tropics and there are a large number of species worldwide.

There are 12 species of hard corals in British and Irish waters of which only one, *Caryophyllia smithii* Devonshire Cup Coral, is common. We have included seven of the species in this book. All of the others, *Balanophyllia celluosa*, *Leptopsammia britannica*, *Flabellum macandrewi*, *Stenocyanthus vermiformis* and *Dendrophyllia cornigera* are deepwater species.

Of the species included, five are solitary corals and only two colonial corals. One of these, *Hoplangia durotrix*, is very small and does not contribute to reef formation. The other, *Lophelia pertusa*, is a cold water coral which, together with other corals, forms substantial reefs in very deep waters.

Caryophyllia smithii Devonshire Cup Coral

Unlike *Corynactis viridis*, clusters of *Caryophyllia smithii* are often of mixed colours. Rathlin, Northern Ireland.

Of all the hard corals this is the most common and widespread. Despite its name this solitary coral is found not just in Devon but around most of the British and Irish coasts. It grows up to 3cm across and occurs in a variety of jewel-like colours, often with a zigzag of contrasting colour around the centre, and a white knob on the end of each transparent tentacle. When fully expanded *Caryophyllia smithii* is easily mistaken for an anemone but when the tentacles are withdrawn the white calcareous 'cup' is obvious. It grows attached to rocks and on shipwrecks from the low water mark

Side view showing barnacles attached to the hard cup. Devon.

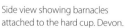

down to at least 100m. In some cases there are one or several tiny barnacles, *Megatrema anglicum*, growing on the side of the cup and distorting its shape.

KEY FEATURES Hard skeleton, knobbed end to each translucent tentacle.

SIMILAR TO Other solitary corals, *Leptopsammia pruvoti* (see p. 142) and *Balanophyllia regia* (see p. 144), have yellow tentacles. *Caryophyllia inornata* (see p. 140) is much smaller and rounder. *Corynactis viridis* (see p. 135) is also brightly coloured and has knobbed tentacles, but does not have a hard skeleton.

Above: Mixed animal turf of *Caryophyllia smithii* with *Actinothoe sphyrodeta*, sponges and bryozoans. Antrim Skerries, Northern Ireland.

Caryophyllia smithii var. *clavus* is a deepwater variety with a very narrow base and can occur living loose in gravel. South Uist.

Caryophyllia inornata Southern Cup Coral

A cluster of *Caryophyllia inornata* with tentacles extended. Plymouth Sound.

This small coral forms solitary cups less than 1cm across and often taller than they are wide. It is much smaller than *Caryophyllia smithii* and is circular rather elliptical in shape. It has knobbed, transparent or plain coloured tentacles. When the hard skeleton is visible it can be seen there are six prominent septa. Although it is a solitary coral it is often found in small compact groups of individuals.

Caryophyllia inornata is probably under-recorded because of confusion with *C. smithii* and the two species can often be seen together. Most records come from south-west England. It is listed as a Priority Species in Scotland and Northern Ireland where it is rare.

KEY FEATURES Small pale circular cup coral.

SIMILAR TO Smaller than *C. smithii* (see p. 138) and circular rather than elliptical when seen from above. Dense groups can look as if they are colonial and thus confused with *Hoplangia durotrix* (see p. 141) which also has a southerly distribution.

Corals with tentacles retracted showing the shape of the corallum. Plymouth, Devon.

Hoplangia durotrix Weymouth Carpet Coral

A cluster of *Hoplangia durotrix* on an overhanging piece of concrete wreckage. Outer Mulberry, Sussex.

This rare colonial coral forms clusters up to 5cm across. It grows well hidden in caves and crevices out of the light from low water down to around 25m. It is thought to only feed at night. It has a restricted south-westerly distribution.

KEY FEATURES Clusters of small circular corallites. Our only shallow water colonial coral.

SIMILAR TO Its appearance is very similar to *Caryophyllia inornata* (p. 140) but the clusters are much more closely fused together with a common base, though this is not always visible. The septa of *Hoplangia durotrix* do not extend beyond the line of the column, giving a very precise rounded appearance to each corallite in the colony.

Sphenotrochus andrewianus Wedge Coral

This is the smallest of all the cup corals and as such is easily overlooked. It grows unattached in coarse sand or shingle and has a wedge shaped cup that only reaches 12mm in length when fully grown. Little is known about the colour of this coral's polyp but it is thought to have up to 24 knobbed tentacles. The juvenile of this species sometimes has a crown of tentacles at both ends of the cup. *Sphenotrochus andrewianus* has been recorded in the past around all of Britain and Ireland but there is only one record in the National Biodiversity Network, from mid Wales. It lives from around 9m down to at least 100m.

KEY FEATURES Tiny, free-living coral.

SIMILAR TO *Caryophyllia smithii* var. *clavus* (p. 139) may also be free living but is much larger.

A cluster of *Leptopsammia pruvoti*. Both *Caryophyllia smithii* and *C. inornata* can be seen above the larger *L. pruvoti*. Sark, Channel Islands.

Leptopsammia pruvoti is the largest and most striking of all the cup corals, and also one of the rarest. It grows to 5cm across and is an intense golden yellow or orange colour. There are 96 tentacles, each with a more intensely coloured tip on the end.

L. *pruvoti* is known only from a few sites in England: the Isles of Scilly, Lundy, south Devon and Lyme Bay. In the Channel Islands and adjacent French waters it is less rare and may occur beneath

overhangs at shallower depths. Though *L. pruvoti* is a solitary coral it is often found in groups of between ten and several hundred individuals. Long-term studies have shown that this slow-growing coral can live to be over 100 years old but reproduces very infrequently making it vulnerable to disturbance. This, and its rarity, have caused it to be listed as a Priority Species in England.

Like other cup corals, the barnacle *Megatrema anglicum* is commonly found attached to the corallum, as in the picture from Lyme Bay. Two worms, the Horseshoe Worm *Phoronis hippocrepia* and a fan worm *Potamilla reniformis* are also known to bore into the base of the corallum and can cause detachment from the rocky surface and hence lead to the death of the coral.

KEY FEATURES Large bright yellow cup coral.

SIMILAR TO Larger than *Balanophyllia regia* (see p. 144), which is the only other yellow cup coral in our waters. *L. pruvoti* is usually found below 20m in shaded places whereas *B. regia* is usually in shallow gullies with surge.

Partly contracted *Leptopsammia pruvoti* showing barnacles *Megatrema anglicum* on the column. Lyme Bay, Dorset.

Balanophyllia regia Scarlet and Gold Star Coral

This is a small cup coral which does not exceed 2.5cm in diameter. It has a deep yellow or orange centre and up to 48 translucent tentacles covered in tiny yellow warts which contain the stinging cells. The tentacles do not have knobs on the end. *Balanophyllia regia* grows in crevices, gullies and on rock faces from the low water mark down to around 25m. Most records are from shallow water, often just below the low tide mark and in areas where there may be considerable surge.

Although this is a solitary cup coral where it does occur there are often a number of individuals close together. In the Channel Islands there appears to be a slightly larger light green form which may be a different species.

KEY FEATURES Small bright yellow cup coral, usually with a darker disk. Limited south-westerly distribution

SIMILAR TO Smaller than *Leptopsammia pruvoti* (see p. 142), which is the only other yellow cup coral in our waters. *B. regia* is usually found in shallow surge gullies, whereas *L. pruvoti* is deeper and in sheltered micro-habitats.

Above: *Balanophyllia regia*. Lizard, Cornwall.
Below: *Balanophyllia regia* In a low tide pool. Lundy, Devon.

Lophelia pertusa Deepwater Coral

The shallowest known *Lophelia pertusa* reef in Europe, in Trondheimsfjord, Norway.

This is by far the largest of all the colonial corals, hard or otherwise, growing in the seas around Britain and Ireland, but as it lives in water between 50–3,000m it is rarely seen.

Lophelia pertusa grows in colonies which can vary enormously in size. Most British and Irish records are of colonies up to 10m in diameter which could be hundreds of years old. However a reef surveyed on the Sula Ridge off Norway in 250m of water was found to be more than 13kms in length and up to 30m high. *L. pertusa* lacks zooxanthellae and thus relies entirely on filtering food from the seawater. Consequently it lives in areas with strong water currents. Because of the large size of the *Lophelia* reefs it has been described as the 'rainforest of the sea' as it provides a rich habitat for many other species of marine life. There are other species of deepwater corals but *L. pertusa* is the only one which might occur within diving depths.

Most British records come from the edge of the Scottish continental shelf, off the Outer Hebrides and west of the Shetlands, as well as around Rockall and to the west of Ireland. However a new reef was discovered in 2004 in the southern part of The Minch between the Scottish mainland and the Outer Hebrides at a depth of between 120–150m. This is the first significant reef recently discovered in British inshore waters. Elsewhere in the North-east Atlantic locations include the narrow areas of some Norwegian fjords. *L. pertusa* also occurs in deep waters in the Mediterranean Sea, along the coasts of eastern North America, Brazil, West Africa and on the mid-Atlantic Ridge. *L. pertusa* has also been known to colonise artificial structures such as the legs of oil rigs.

KEY FEATURES Deepwater (200m plus) reef building coral. Bright white in colour.

SIMILAR SPECIES There are no similar species in shallow waters. *Parazoanthus anguicomus* (p. 64) is a similar colour and has similar polyps but is not a hard coral and does not form reefs. Extensive growths of the Coral Worm, *Salmacina dysteri* have also been mistaken for *L. pertusa* in the past. These do have hard tubes with a fan of tentacles on each, but are much smaller and are not corals.

Deepwater coral reefs

Reef building corals are very rare in shallow waters around Britain and Ireland. However we do have deepwater coral reefs far offshore on the edge of the continental shelf.

The main reef building coral is *Lophelia pertusa* (p. 145) but there are a large number of other scleractinian corals, lace corals (Stylasteridae), black corals (antipatharians), soft corals and sea fans (gorgonians). *Madrepora oculata* is the second most common coral. Sometimes known as the Zigzag Coral, it is one of only 12 deepwater coral species found worldwide, including in the sub-Antarctic. It is much less robust than *Lophelia*.

Deepwater coral reefs attract fishes and since the 1980s large-scale fishing operations have targeted deepwater populations as stocks of shallow water species have declined. Photographic and acoustic surveys have located trawl marks in depths of up to 1,400m on the North-east Atlantic shelf edge off Ireland, Scotland and Norway. The trawl scars are up to 4km long and characterised by parallel trenches where heavy fishing gear designed to keep nets close to the seabed has damaged sessile marine life, dragged rocks and turned over sediment. Whilst fishermen try to avoid the coral reefs themselves, as they can severely damage their gear, collateral damage does occur and it is likely that large areas of these slow growing fragile reefs have been reduced to rubble.

Lophelia coral reef west of Ireland damaged by deepwater fishing activity. (© *Söffker et al.*).

Both the UK and Ireland have recognised the problem and have identified large areas of deepwater reefs as Special Areas of Conservation under the EU Habitats Directive.

The Hatton Bank (1) is the furthest offshore and is a volcanic bank 500km in length with depths varying from 500–100m. It has been a candidate SAC since 2013. Two other candidate SACs with coral reefs were submitted at the same time and were designated in 2017, East Rockall Bank (3) and the Anton Dohrn Seamount (4). The latter has clumps of Lophelia reef at the top of the seamount in 530m, but there are steep cliffs around the sides to 2,400m.

The largest known cold water coral reef in UK waters is the North-west Rockall Bank (2). This is 450km in length and 200km wide and has coral reef growing over cobbles and pebbles at depths of between 200–1,000m. It was also designated as an SAC in 2017. The most northerly of the coral reef SACs is the Darwin Mounds (5) which lie 160km north of Cape Wrath. Here there are sandy mounds capped with *Lophelia* reef, each one about 100m in diameter and 5m high. It was designated an SAC in 2015.

In Irish waters the three Special Areas of Conservation containing cold water corals are North-west Porcupine Bank (6), Hovland Mound Province (7) and South-west Porcupine Bank (8). These are all carbonate mounds in depths of 400–1,600m, with the mounds themselves up to 200m high and capped with *Lophelia* reef. These were all designated as SACs in 2016.

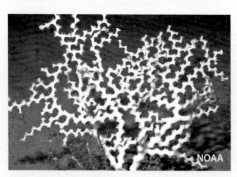

Madrepora oculata Zigzag Coral.

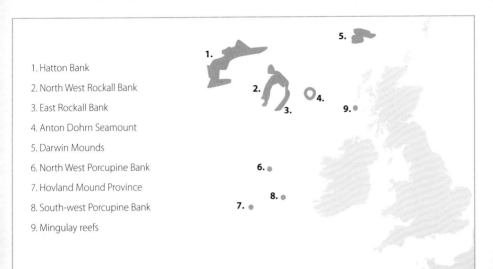

1. Hatton Bank
2. North West Rockall Bank
3. East Rockall Bank
4. Anton Dohrn Seamount
5. Darwin Mounds
6. North West Porcupine Bank
7. Hovland Mound Province
8. South-west Porcupine Bank
9. Mingulay reefs

Cold water coral reef Special Areas of Conservation in British and Irish waters.

Special Area of Conservation status does not in itself result in management of damaging activities. Regulations to control fishing need to be brought in by the competent authority, which in these far offshore sites is normally the European Commission. Only two of the SACs are subject to a ban on bottom fishing, The Darwin Mounds (5) have been closed since 2003 and most of the North-west Rockall Bank (2) since 2008. The other areas remain open for fishing.

The only known inshore cold water coral reef is east of Mingulay in the Outer Hebrides (9). This was first discovered in 2003 and lies in depths of 100–200m. Because it is relatively shallow, this reef has

Fishes are attracted to *Lophelia* reefs, here *Sebastes marinus* on Europe's shallowest cold water reef in Throndheimsfjord, Norway at 45m.

been the subject of much study and over 350 different species have been recorded, including 100 sponges alone. It was proposed as a Site of Community Importance in 2011 but has not yet been formally designated and there is currently no scheme in place for its management.

References
Trawling damage to Northeast Atlantic ancient coral reefs
Jason Hall-Spencer, Valerie Allain and Jan Helge Fossa. 2002. *Proc. R. Soc. Lond. B* 269, 507–511.
In situ observations of fish associated with coral reefs off Ireland.
Söffker M., Sloman K.A., and Hall-Spencer J.M. 2011. *Deep-Sea Research* Part 1 58, 818–825.

Websites
www.lophelia.org An information resource on the cold-water coral ecosystems of the deep ocean.

For information on the conservation status in UK and Ireland:
www.jncc.defra.gov.uk/page-6895 (UK offshore SACs); **www.snh.gov.uk** (Mingulay)
www.npws.ie/protected-sites/sac (Ireland).

Conservation of sea anemones and corals in Britain and Ireland

Much publicity has been given to human and climate change impacts on tropical coral reefs, many of which are in serious decline. There are also conservation issues for temperate water corals and anemones.

Cold water reef-building corals

The only reef-building corals in British and Irish seas are in very deep water on the edge of the continental shelf. Here the *Lophelia* reefs were for many years too deep to be affected by human activities. However overfishing of shallow water fish stocks and the use of larger fishing vessels have led to an expansion of deep water fisheries and in particular bottom trawling. This has the potential of destroying extensive areas of deep water reef over a short period. For more information see pp. 146–147.

Biodiversity Action Plans

As a part of its response to the Rio Earth Summit the UK government established an action planning process aimed at maintaining habitat and species diversity. The resulting biodiversity action plans (BAPs) operated both at a national and local level. The list of species was augmented in 2007 and Seasearch studies have contributed to our knowledge of a number of the BAP species.

The UK Post-2010 Biodiversity Framework, published in July 2012, has now succeeded the UK BAP. In particular, due to devolution and the creation of country-level biodiversity strategies, much of the work previously carried out under the UK BAP is now focussed at a country level.

The UK BAP lists of priority species and habitats remain, however, important and valuable reference sources. Notably, they have been used to help draw up statutory lists of priorities covering England, Wales, Scotland and Northern Ireland.

Inclusion in a Priority Species list does not confer any protection on the species concerned. Effective protection would have to be achieved through inclusion within a Marine Protected Area, under the Wildlife and Countryside Act or through fisheries and other specific legislation.

Whilst there are relatively few marine species in the Priority Species lists, anemones and corals are prominently represented. The species are:

		England	Wales	Scotland	Northern Ireland
Slender Sea Pen	Virgularia mirabilis				y
Pink Sea Fan	Eunicella verrucosa	y	y		
Northern Sea Fan	Swiftia pallida			y	
Tall Sea Pen	Funiculina quadrangularis	y		y	
Fireworks Anemone	Pachycerianthus multiplicatus			y	
	Arachnanthus sarsi			y	y
Sea Fan Anemone	Amphianthus dohrnii	y		y	
Yellow Cluster Anemone	Parazoanthus axinellae			y	y
Starlet Sea Anemone	Nematostella vectensis	y			
Ivell's Anemone	Edwardsia ivelli	y			
	Edwardsia timida	y	y	y	y
Southern Cup Coral	Caryophyllia inornata			y	y
Sunset Cup Coral	Leptopsammia pruvoti	y			

The **Pink Sea Fan** *Eunicella verrucosa*, the **Sea Fan Anemone** *Amphianthus dohrnii* (which lives on it) and the **Sunset Cup Coral** *Leptopsammia pruvoti* are all characteristic species of south-westerly rocky reefs. The Pink Sea Fan and Sunset Cup Coral are both long-lived species whose presence on a reef demonstrates stability in the conditions they need to survive over a number of decades. On the other hand little is known about the biology of the Sea Fan Anemone, though Seasearch is contributing to the knowledge base by recording occurrences through its sea fan recording programme, and through the specific study described on page 131.

The Sea Fan Anemone and Sunset Cup Coral are both categorised as nationally rare species whilst the Pink Sea Fan is nationally scarce. Sea fans were collected in the 1960 and 70s as souvenirs and it is consequently one of very few marine species protected from intentional damage or disturbance by the Wildlife and Countryside Act.

Pink Sea Fan skeletons amongst netting. Chesil Beach, Dorset.

Collection as souvenirs has ceased but the species faces a much bigger threat from bottom trawling and entanglement in monofilament fishing nets. This has led to a ban on bottom fishing over reefs in Lyme Bay where the extent of damage to sea fan populations was shown to be extremely high. Prior to this ban after winter storms large numbers of sea fans were regularly washed up tangled in netting on Chesil Bank at the eastern end of Lyme Bay.

Seasearch studies have shown that the highest incidence of Sea Fan Anemones is on sea fans at the Manacles on the Lizard peninsula in Cornwall. Part of this area has been designated as a Marine Conservation Zone (see below) and Seasearch has recommended its extension to cover more of the sea fan habitat.

There are also three characteristically northern species the **Northern Sea Fan** *Swiftia pallida*, **Tall Sea Pen** *Funiculina quadrangularis* and **Fireworks Anemone** *Pachycerianthus multiplicatus*. All of these species have been the focus of Seasearch surveys in western Scotland. All three species are thought to have been badly affected by bottom fishing with scampi or prawn trawling particularly affecting Tall Sea Pens and Fireworks Anemones which live in the same muddy habitat. *Aracnanthus sarsi* and *Edwardsia timida* are also sediment dwelling species and subject to the same pressures.

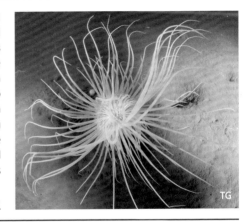

Firework Anemones are a priority species in Scotland.

The **Starlet Sea Anemone** *Nematostella vectensis* and **Ivell's Anemone** *Edwardsia ivelli* are both brackish water, lagoonal, species. They are therefore extremely vulnerable to loss of habitat from development activities or localised pollution effects. It is quite possible that Ivell's Anemone has become extinct as it was only known from a single lagoon in West Sussex where it has not been found for some years. Most of the sites where the Starlet Sea Anemone occurs are designated as Sites of Special Scientific Interest. However one of the actions in the BAP for this species was to increase the number of sites where they are found by habitat creation.

Marine Protected Areas (MPAs)

1. Marine Nature Reserves

The legal basis in the UK for the establishment of Marine Nature Reserves (MNRs) was the Wildlife and Countryside Act 1981. In over 25 years since the legislation was passed only three MNRs were established, Lundy in Devon, Skomer in south Wales and Strangford Lough in Northern Ireland.

Of the anemone and coral BAP species Pink Sea Fans are found in two of the three MNRs, Lundy and Skomer, and Sunset Cup Corals are also found at Lundy. Sadly, work carried out by the Marine Conservation Society and Seasearch has shown that populations of both species have declined at Lundy.

The MNR legislation did not allow fishing activity to be controlled in Marine Nature Reserves. That would have to be done by Sea Fisheries Committee Bylaws and it was not until 2004 that part of Lundy was made a statutory no take zone. However it is unlikely that the level of fishing at either Lundy or Skomer is having any adverse effect on the sea fans and cup corals.

Active monitoring takes place at Skomer which includes the sea fan populations. The monitoring around Lundy has been more diverse with a mixture of surveys undertaken on behalf of the statutory authorities, by the wardens and by volunteers.

Both Lundy and Skomer are now Marine Conservation Zones.

In Ireland Nature Reserves are designated under the Wildlife Act of 1976. Lough Hyne in Co. Cork was designated in 1981 and was the first marine nature reserve in Britain and Ireland.

2. Special Areas of Conservation (SACs)

European Union member states have an obligation to identify Special Areas of Conservation (SACs) arising from the EU Habitats Directive. There is a requirement to monitor biodiversity in these areas and to act to protect them.

In the UK a number of the SACs cover reef areas and include sites where the Pink Sea Fan, Sea Fan Anemone and Sunset Cup Coral all occur, such as the Isles of Scilly, Lyme Bay, Plymouth and Lundy.

Ireland has a number of SACs for reefs in which the Pink Sea Fan occurs. The Valentia Harbour/Portmagee Channel SAC has the very rare anemone *Edwardsia delapiae*. This anemone has not been found anywhere else and is Ireland's only known marine endemic species. Kilkieran Bay and Islands SAC in Galway has Ireland's only population of Fireworks Anemones

Offshore SACs to protect deepwater coral reefs are listed on pp. 146–147.

3. Marine Conservation Zones (MCZs)

Legislation has been passed in England, Wales, Scotland and Northern Ireland to create national designations for marine protected areas. These are known as Marine Conservation Zones (MCZs) in England, Wales and Northern Ireland and Marine Protected Areas (MPAs) in Scotland. There have been two tranches of designations in England covering over 50 sites, 30 sites designated in Scotland and 4 in Northern Ireland. Priority species such as Pink and Northern Sea Fans featured in the selection process and are identified as features to be maintained in a favourable condition in a number of the MCZs and MPAs.

Pink Sea Fans are a feature of reef SACs in south-west England as here at the Eddystone, Devon.

Other conservation measures

Sites of Special Scientific Interest (SSSIs) are commonly used on land to protect important habitats and species. However they cannot extend below low water mark and are therefore not generally appropriate for marine sites. Enclosed lagoons and intertidal areas can be included and many of the locations where Starlet Sea Anemones occur are SSSIs. There is no equivalent legislation at present to protect areas below the low water mark.

Three of the British anemones and corals are also protected species under the Wildlife and Countryside Act. The two lagoonal species, the Starlet Sea Anemone and Ivell's Anemone, became protected in 1988 and the Pink Sea Fan, in 1992. This means that it is offence to kill, injure, take, possess or offer these animals for sale.

In Ireland Natural Heritage Areas (NHAs) can be designated under the Wildlife (Amendment) Act 2000 and a number of marine areas were proposed as NHAs including Roaringwater Bay and Islands SAC in Co. Cork. To date no marine sites have been formally designated.

Biosecurity and non-native species

The only non-native invasive anemone species in British and Irish waters is the Orange-striped Green Anemone *Diadumene lineata*, page 103. It is not widely recorded and is not currently a significant problem. Scuba divers, along with other sea users, have a part to play in preventing the spread of non-native species. Some of these may be nuisance or invasive species (INNS, invasive non-native species). If you suspect that you have been diving in water containing one of these then WHEREVER POSSIBLE the Check-Clean-Dry guidelines at www.nonnativespecies.org/checkcleandry (in Ireland see www.invasivespeciesireland.com/biosecurity) should be followed. Photographs of the possible INNS should be taken *in situ*, taking care not to disturb or dislodge, and a report made of the sighting (you can send an email to alertnonnative@ceh.ac.uk).

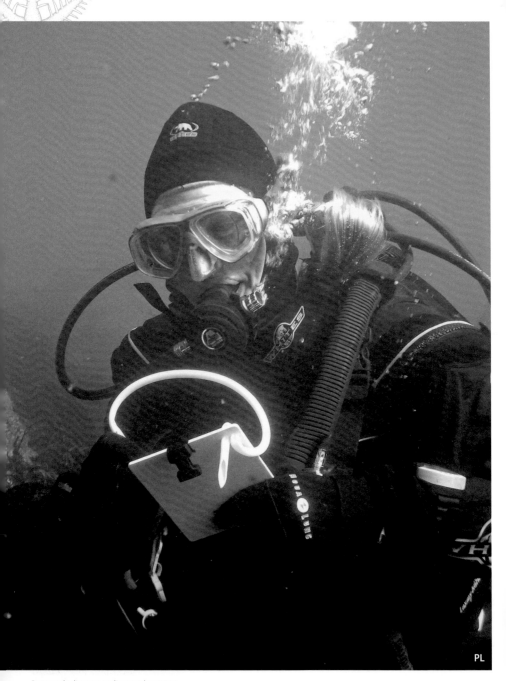

Seasearch diver recording underwater.

Seasearch diving and recording

This guide has been produced mainly to help Seasearch divers and snorkellers with identification of the sea anemones and corals they see on their dives. We hope it will also lead to more records of species which divers have not previously been able to recognise.

Seasearch is a volunteer underwater survey project for recreational divers throughout Britain and Ireland to record observations of marine habitats and the life they support. The information gathered is used to increase our knowledge of the marine environment and contribute towards its conservation.

Seasearch data has helped to define the boundaries of areas for conservation, recorded the presence of rare and unusual species and provided information for local groups to campaign for protection of their local marine life and habitats. The data are held both by local record centres and centrally and are available for anyone to consult on the internet through the National Biodiversity Network (NBN). Go to **www.nbn.org.uk** to see it.

Divers can participate in Seasearch training courses at different levels suitable to their knowledge and experience. These include the Observer Course which gives an introduction to marine habitat and species identification and survey methods. The Surveyor Course is for more experienced recorders and there are also Specialist Courses which provide participants with more information on specific groups of marine life or additional survey techniques.

In addition to a national coordinator for the project, there is also a network of local coordinators in many coastal areas who organise Seasearch survey dives and training. We can also provide training and talks in other areas on demand. For further information see the Seasearch web site at

www.seasearch.org.uk

Seasearch is co-ordinated by the Marine Conservation Society on behalf of the Seasearch Supporters which comprise the Marine Conservation Society, Wildlife Trusts, Joint Nature Conservation Committee, Natural England, Natural Resources Wales, Scottish Natural Heritage, Department of the Environment Northern Ireland, Environment Agency, Marine Biological Association, British Sub Aqua Club, Sub Aqua Association, Professional Association of Diving Instructors, Scottish Sub Aqua Club and Irish Underwater Council. Seasearch receives financial support from some of the organisations above.

Seasearch hopes that this guide will encourage even more divers to complete Seasearch forms after any of their sea dives. You can download Seasearch forms from our website or obtain them from any of the coordinators.

Any dive can be a Seasearch dive!

RMo

Books and websites

BOOKS

British Anthozoa, Key Notes for the Identification of the Species Manuel, R.L. 1981. Linnean Society of London.
A complete review of British Anthozoa and the source of much of the information in this book. Also contains detailed information on each species and is illustrated by beautiful line drawings. There is an extensive bibliography. As this work is over 35 years old there are inevitably some changes in nomenclature that have occurred subsequently.

The Anthozoa of the British Isles – a colour guide R. L. Manuel. 1980. Underwater Conservation Society.
Long unavailable this 'miniprint guide' was the first attempt to provide information and colour pictures of British Anthozoa to help the marine naturalist. It has been an important source of information and I hope this book will be as useful to readers in the future as my dog eared copy of the guide has been to me in the past.

Actinologica Britannica: A History of the British Sea-anemones and corals P. H. Gosse. 1860. Van Voorst, London.
The first review of the British Sea anemones and corals and the source of many of the original descriptions of the species. Whilst many of the names have subsequently changed and a number of species have been combined or separated, it is astonishing how much had been described 150 years ago, long before the advent of the diving surveys that have allowed us to see many of these species in their natural habitats.

Hydroids, Sea Anemones, Jellyfish and Comb Jellies Cornelius P.F.S., Manuel, R.L., Ryland, J.S., Schuchert, P. and Wood, C. *In* Handbook of the Marine Fauna of North-West Europe, Second Edition. Edited by P. J. Hayward and J. S. Ryland. Oxford University Press 2017.
Recently revised and extended version of this classic handbook. Illustrated primarily with line drawings.

There are a number of general field guides which contain a selection of the sea anemones and corals found in this book. They are a useful source of additional photographs as so often looking at more than one image can help with identification. I list a small selection of recent guides that I have found useful.

Great British Marine Animals 3rd Edition Paul Naylor. 2011. Sound Diving Publications, Plymouth.

Marine Fish and Invertebrates of Northern Europe Frank Emil Moen and Erling Svensen. 2004. Kom, Norway and Aquapress, Southend on Sea.

Diver's Guide to Marine Life of Britain and Ireland Chris Wood. 2013. Wild Nature Press, Plymouth.

Marine Life of the Channel Islands Sue Daly. 1998. Kingdom Books, Waterlooville.

Sussex Marine Life – an identification guide for divers Robert Irving. 1998. Sussex Seasearch.

WEBSITES

Encyclopedia of Marine Life of Britain and Ireland
www.habitas.org.uk/marinelife

Based in the Ulster Museum and maintained by Bernard Picton and Christine Morrow, this photographic guide covers a selection of the larger animals which live round the coasts of Britain and Ireland. It is intended for divers and marine biologists who need to be able to recognise species *in situ* and is illustrated by underwater pictures. It is a good source for updated information on species and contains other images of almost all of the anemones and corals included in this book.

MarLIN The Marine Life Information Network for Britain and Ireland
www.marlin.ac.uk

Based at the Marine Biological Association in Plymouth the site contains *Biodiversity and Conservation for Key Species*. These provide much information about the selected species, including many of the species in this book. There are photographs of all of the species included.

Joint Nature Conservation Committee
www.jncc.defra.gov.uk/marine

The marine section of the site contains information on protected sites, habitats and species and includes the *Marine Habitat Classification for the UK* which is used in professional level surveys.

National Biodiversity Network – NBN Atlas
www.nbn.org.uk

This site allows you to view distribution maps and download UK wildlife data by using a variety of interactive tools. This is the public repository for all Seasearch information and has the benefit that you can search for marine data from a number of sources on a single search.

Seasearch
www.seasearch.org.uk

The site for all the information about Seasearch and how to take part. You can download recording forms and guidance and find out what courses and diving surveys are planned in your area. The site also gives access to over 300 reports of surveys.

Seasearch Identifications and NE Atlantic Cnidaria
www.facebook.com/groups/seasearch.identifications
www.facebook.com/groups/224626804295339/?fref=ts

Facebook groups for those interested in Identifying unusual species where you are likely to get an authoritative answer from active diver-recorders.

WoRMS – World Register of Marine Species
www.marinespecies.org

The aim of a World Register of Marine Species (WoRMS) is to provide an authoritative and comprehensive list of names of marine organisms, including information on synonymy. It is the most reliable source for up to date scientific names and has been used in this second edition to update some of the names in the first edition.

Taxonomic list of Anthozoan species in Britain and Ireland included in this guide

Phylum Cnidaria
Superclass Anthozoa
Class Octocorallia

Class Hexacorallia

Index

Page entries in **bold** refer to the main species accounts.